# Volunteers Wanted

*A Practical Guide
to Finding and Keeping
Good Volunteers*

## Jo B. Rusin

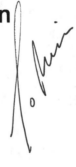

**Magnolia
Mansions
Press**

Volunteers Wanted
A Practical Guide to Finding and Keeping Good Volunteers
Copyright © 1999 by Jo Bryan Rusin.

FIRST EDITION
First Printing, 1999

ISBN 0-9665175-2-0

LCCN: 99-61522

Cover art and design by Carolyn Miller Design

Magnolia Mansions Press
A Division of BOCO Industries
4661 Pinewood Drive
Mobile, Alabama 36618
boellis@aol.com

*To Margaret Boland Ellis*
*without whose encouragement and support*
*this book would still be just a good idea.*

# CONTENTS

## APPENDICES

# Preface

As a volunteer and leader of volunteers for 33 years, I have worked with a variety of programs, some more effective than others. Nearly everyone I know is now or has at some time been a volunteer. A few have considered volunteering, but then decided not to do so. Just as there is no one ideal volunteer, there is no ideal program. However, successful volunteer programs have many characteristics in common in how they recruit, employ, and retain their volunteers. There are worthy volunteer programs all over America struggling to find and keep good people. My goal in this book is to share my collective experience and that gleaned from friends, fellow volunteers, and volunteer program managers on what works and what doesn't work. No one should have to spend years of trial and error to learn the basics of leading and motivating volunteers. This book cannot cover every situation, of course. Rather it is hoped that through studying the basics and practical examples, leaders of volunteers and volunteer program managers will be able to design programs that fit their particular situation.

In writing this book, I am deeply indebted to many friends who have generously shared their experiences. More good people have helped than I could possibly list here. However, I would like to particularly thank Margaret Boland Ellis, Geraldine Wright, Clay and Betty Smith, Liz Ruffin, Simmie Walker, Dr. Leon McGaughey, General Ed Burba, Trish Burba, Maggie Siegfried, Greg and Nikki Wheeler, Priscilla Spraggs, Joetta Rusin, Jean Bryan, and especially my husband, Johnny Rusin. Without their insight and constructive criticism, this book would be simply one person's perspective.

NOTE: The examples in this book name a number of well known volunteer organizations. For purpose of illustration some examples are positive while others are negative. The examples are not intended as generalizations about the organization named nor do the examples imply any reflection on the integrity of the organization as a whole. Major organizations have been selected for examples because they are volunteer programs with which many people have had experience and can identify.

Although based on experience, names used in the examples are pseudonyms and in some cases the circumstances have been modified to prevent potential embarrassment for the actual person or persons involved.

# 1

# THE PRICELESS RESOURCE

**Volunteers are priceless.** While paid workers may or may not be highly motivated , volunteers are working for your program because they want to be there. They care about what you are doing and have a level of motivation which cannot be bought. Properly encouraged and developed, their efforts continue to grow over time. Some volunteers will work only a day or a few weeks, which may be all you want. Others will stay with the program and eventually become its backbone. Volunteers bring unique skills, experience, and energy.

Volunteers are as varied as humanity itself and the sky is the limit on who you recruit for your program - you don't need to have money to pay them. Volunteers are valuable and must be treated as such. After all, even though they don't cost money, they aren't cheap. Who are these valuable people who volunteer? Volunteers are your friends, your neighbors, and anyone in the community with the energy and skills you need who you can interest in your program. They are young, old, male, female, single, married, divorced, have children, childless, in school, working, retired, and of all races and ethnic backgrounds. Each volunteer is an individual and each has special gifts to bring to your program. Let's look at a sample of people who do volunteer.

## Examples

➤ Ed is a retiree with a college degree in electrical engineering and thirty- five years of experience in manufacturing and sales. He has been a Boy Scout troop leader and has spent many hours volunteering with Habitat for Humanity. Ed is now a Habitat for Humanity project site manager. In addition, Ed also volunteers with a wildlife rescue program and as a blacksmith at a local historic site.

➤ Ruth is a high school principal, who is active in her community and church. As a volunteer, she has been a guide for the Olympic Games, tutors elementary school children with reading problems, and leads an academic enrichment program for children at her church during the summer.

➤ Roger is a brick mason, who is still involved with his neighborhood school even though his children are now grown. He volunteers in the evening and on weekends to help the custodial staff and to make minor repairs at the school. Last year Roger donated and built a new masonry sign for the school's front entrance.

➤ Suzanne is a business woman and published author on the problems of aging. She is married and has a teenage daughter. Although she travels often to give presentations on aging, Suzanne also volunteers as a Girl Scout troop leader.

➤ John is a veterinarian, who has volunteered as a reading tutor since he was in college. His schedule and family responsibilities restrict his time now. Still, he enjoys helping young people to read and continues tutoring twice a month at a Salvation Army family shelter.

➤ Erica is a certified public accountant, who works as a financial advisor for an international banking company. Because of her love of dogs, she and her husband began volunteering at their county humane society. Erica is now the treasurer for the humane society, as well as helping at adoption days.

**Volunteering is about inclusion.** It is about being part of an organization doing good work that is larger than yourself. As part of a team, volunteers can contribute far more than they can as individuals. They must be made to feel a part of the team despite their individual differences.

➤ Ashley is a full time wife and mother, although she has cerebral palsy. She is an active volunteer with her church's outreach program and is in charge of the nursery on Sunday mornings.

➤ Reginald is a high school senior who has volunteered for two years with Habitat for Humanity. He started volunteering after his own family was flooded out of their home and was assisted in rebuilding by volunteers. A talented and energetic worker, Reginald is now a crew leader.

➤ Eugenia is the mother of two teenagers. She has been a volunteer room mother and is now a library volunteer at her sons' school. In addition, Eugenia volunteers two evenings a month at an downtown soup kitchen. A lifelong speech impediment has not stopped Eugenia from being an outstanding volunteer.

➤ Mike teaches at a school for deaf children. He has masters degrees in Special Education Management, Emotional Disturbance and Behavior Disorders, and Physical Education. As a father, he volunteered with Cub

Scouts and Boy Scouts. He is now a volunteer soccer coach for two teams. Mike's teams are the only ones in the county which take multi-handicapped and deaf children.

➤ Cheryl is a hairdresser, who volunteers two Saturdays a month to shampoo and cut hair for invalids who cannot leave their homes to have their hair done. She began volunteering with Meals on Wheels and enjoyed her work, but saw a need for this kind of personal service. When she offered to expand her work, the Meals on Wheels program coordinator saw the potential and referred her to the community hospice program with which she now volunteers.

➤ Anthony was the senior staff member in customer relations for the telephone company before he was medically retired. He now volunteers several days a week with a debt counseling service where his conflict resolution skills and ability to listen have been invaluable.

➤ Ariel is a retired college professor, who also worked as a librarian with a federal agency. She is fluent in Spanish and English. Ariel has volunteered in a number of programs and is currently very active as a Eucharistic minister and lay reader in her parish.

➤ Jeremy and Keith are mentally disabled adults, having the mental capacity of about 10 and 12 year old children. They and their parents are active in their church where Jeremy and Keith serve as ushers for Sunday services. Both men are known and liked by the congregation, as they are exceptionally reliable and conscientious in their duties.

➤ Martha is a widow whose children are now grown and have moved away. She is a former newspaper reporter, customer service agent, high school teacher, writer, and private pilot. A versatile and busy individual, she volunteers her time on several advisory panels. Martha also volunteers each summer at the local YWCA camp to teach nature study and crafts.

**Volunteers' qualifications are not always obvious in the beginning.** Unlike paid employees, volunteers don't submit resumes. In fact, new volunteers who arrive with lists of credentials and experience are often suspect. And sometimes what people say they can do and what they do best are not the same thing, such as the volunteer who said he was an expert finishing carpenter. While he was a hard working volunteer, he was not an expert carpenter. You must discover what a volunteer does best and where his skills lie through graduated involvement in the program and getting to know him as an individual. And like all living things, volunteers' skills grow and develop as they are cultivated and nurtured.

**Every volunteer has gifts to offer.** Along with those gifts, they are giving you their time and energy. Even if you could find paid employees with the skills volunteers bring, few organizations could afford to pay them what they are worth. And most volunteers are not looking for a forty hour week, although some work that and more depending upon the job. Your challenge is to give them a fulfilling job they enjoy and to make them an integral part of your program. The volunteer talent is there if you will look for and develop it. While there may be individual exceptions, overall volunteers represent the best society has to offer.

# 2

# WHAT DO VOLUNTEERS COST?

**Volunteers are not free labor.** While it is true volunteers do not get paid, a successful volunteer program requires an up front commitment of resources, time and energy. If the staff administering the program is paid or there are advertising costs, financial resources will also be necessary. The success of a volunteer program is directly proportional to the amount of resources, energy, and time the organization devotes to its volunteers. Deciding to implement a new volunteer program or fine tune an existing one is no small task. Management must be prepared to expend the resources necessary. A volunteer program operated cheaply can be worse than no volunteer program because of the poor public relations image it creates. Having said this, what are the costs?

**Commitment.** The organization must be fully committed to the use and value of volunteers from the very top level of management. While it may take a while to sway those at the lower levels of the organization, everyone in management must want volunteers to participate. This is less of a challenge in organizations composed exclusively of volunteers than it is in nonprofit groups with paid staffs and in the public sector, for example schools and libraries. Paid staff members may see volunteers as a threat to their jobs or their power in the organization. They may consciously or unconsciously sabotage the use of volunteers. In a similar fashion, long time volunteers may resist the inclusion of new volunteers fearing the loss of their position or control. The boss and subordinate leaders must want volunteers and must speak out in favor of them.

### Example

The superintendent of schools has recently instituted a program to involve senior citizens in the community in a tutoring program in the city schools. Malcolm, the Oakley Middle School Principal, has worked hard to improve structure and discipline at his school both among students and faculty. He does not want a bunch of volunteers coming into his school interrupting the school day and he especially doesn't want a bunch of retirees telling him how to run his school. Rather than discuss this with the superintendent, he solves the problem himself. Whenever people call his school to volunteer, the office staff is instructed to ask them what days and times they can tutor. They are then told that no tutors are needed at those times. Those who say they can come at any time are told someone will get back with them. Of course, no one ever calls them back. As a result, there are no volunteers at Oakley Middle School.

The decision to use volunteers needs to be well coordinated within the organization and all leaders have to be committed to its success. In addition, as many workers as possible must support the decision.

**Time and Energy.** Implementing and operating volunteer programs are time and energy intensive, both in the initial recruitment and placement phases and the subsequent development of the program. In addition to the paper work of designing and advertising, time must be spent talking to people in person and on the telephone as the program comes together. Teaching new volunteers and coaching experienced volunteers take worker time. To ignore this time requirement is to build in mediocrity, if not failure. Even with existing volunteer programs, the volunteer program coordinator and volunteer supervisors must devote time and energy to coaching and thanking volunteers. Giving feedback to volunteers is essential to making them integrated members of the team. For a paid staff member, adding the title Volunteer Coordinator means a major increase in responsibility and time. It is not an additional duty to be taken lightly.

**Money**. Depending on how elaborate your volunteer program is, money must be budgeted and programmed to offset costs. The amount of money depends not only on the funds available, but also on the tone you wish to set. Among the things organizations commonly spend money for are advertising for volunteers, additional equipment for volunteers to use, recognition plaques, and uniforms. The annual volunteer appreciation luncheon can also be an expense. Of course, the luncheon can be a potluck affair, however, this might not be appropriate in all organizations. Supplies for volunteers may be as simple as paper and pens or as elaborate as additional computer terminals. In order to attract and keep volunteers you must also consider costs to support the volunteer, for example, parking and childcare.

### Example

Jack volunteers each Wednesday night at an inner city homeless shelter. Safe parking is at a premium in the area and can cost as much as $10 for the evening. The shelter where he works has set aside spaces in its own leased staff parking area just for volunteers. As a regular volunteer, Jack has a parking sticker for these spaces. Parking here makes it easy for him to continue volunteering at the shelter and to be there on time each week. Coincidentally, his parking sticker also serves as a small advertisement for shelter volunteers.

Don't expect your volunteers to underwrite all the monetary expenses of your volunteer program. After all, they are giving you their time for free. When their out of pocket costs exceed the value they get from volunteering with your program, many volunteers will reach a point where they say, "This just isn't worth it." Unfortunately, they rarely tell you this directly. They will simply stop coming to volunteer.

**Communication**. Volunteers must know what is going on in the organization as well as what they are expected to do as individuals. In smaller organizations, most communication is done over the telephone. This takes time and people willing to make the calls. Newsletters, E-mail, and letters to individuals can also keep volunteers informed. Before sending out information, though, look at it from the volunteer's perspective. Is this actually information volunteers need or would like to know or is it just fanfare for the organization and its staff? The following example is a letter sent to key volunteers.

### Example:

Greetings, fellow volunteers!

I am pleased to announce my acceptance of the honorable position of Chairman of Volunteers. To achieve success, we need the help of each and every volunteer. I hope to follow successfully in the footsteps of outgoing Chairman of Volunteers, Art Bingham, who has held this position since 1995.

There will be an organizational meeting at 12:00 noon Wednesday, September 30, at the main office. The purpose of this meeting is to discuss important issues, such as how to better communicate with, utilize, and recognize volunteers.

You have been recognized for your leadership and commitment to the delivery of valuable services and programs. Please plan to attend this very significant assembly of key volunteers.

From the perspective of the volunteer who received this letter, he must not be very important since the letter is not addressed to him by name, only as "Greetings, fellow volunteers!". The writer spends the whole first paragraph telling about himself and his predecessor. He doesn't get around to telling the volunteer he is being invited because he is a key volunteer until the last two.

Technically, this letter is communication. It is unlikely, however, to solicit the support the writer desires because it does not effectively communicate the value of the volunteer to the organization. Contrast this letter with the next example, an E-mail sent to all volunteers by name. In this case the volunteers are public school tutors.

### Example:

Happy New Year!! Hopefully everyone enjoyed the holidays. I wanted to give you some info on the school for this year:
- The next Citizen of the Month ceremony will be Friday, January 23. Check to see if your student will be honored.
- School will be closed January 19-23 for the Martin Luther King Holiday and April 6-10 for teachers' planning days.
- The school wanted me to let you know on March 16-27

the students will be taking the Iowa Test of Basic Skills. Please do not go over to tutor your child during that week.

• Children are getting ready for the Science Fair, February 6. Check with your child to see of you can work with them on their project.

• Wednesday, January 14, at 10:00 a.m. public relations will be making a video tape of our partnership program to send to send to corporate headquarters. I would love to have all of you on the tape if you can be there. I will also use this tape for briefings in the community, etc. I need your help if you can be there. *Thanks for your kindness. You are special!!!!*

This example gives volunteers information they need to know while at the same time letting them know they are valuable members of the tutoring partnership.

**Flexibility**. When you already have an established way of doing things, adding volunteers or increasing the number of volunteers will require changes and flexibility in people and the organization. Not every volunteer will be capable of nor interested in doing the same job. Not every volunteer will be available to work at the same time. Without flexibility your volunteer program will be greatly restricted. Outstanding potential volunteers will be lost because they cannot be fitted into an inflexible program.

### Example

The Community Food Bank decided to expand its program, primarily because a major wholesale grocery distributor had recently agreed to make large donations of food every two weeks. In the past the program had operated successfully with a small core of volunteers, who worked weekdays to stock shelves and distribute food to clients. Now with the large influx of food, more volunteers were needed. At first the program tried to recruit more volunteers for the existing schedule. Few applied and those who came seemed to get in the way. Finally, three of the experienced volunteers offered to come in two evenings a week and Saturday mornings to supervise and help with the stocking of shelves. This flexibility allowed the organization to expand its recruitment of volunteers and thus its overall program.

Responding to the changes wrought by adding volunteers requires a different way of looking at problems and a willingness to modify existing procedures to incorporate additional workers.

**Risk**. Operating a volunteer program is not for the timid. Accepting volunteers into your organization involves risk. While you are responsible for the work volunteers do, you have less direct control over them than you would have with paid workers. There are ways to reduce the financial risk to the organization (*See Appendix B, Liability and Insurance Considerations.*). Volunteers may be different from your paid staff. They may have new ideas or different ways of doing things. If you are unwilling to accept this risk, then you are concurrently saying no to the tremendous potential for enhancement and improvement offered by volunteers. A decision to commit to the acceptance of volunteers is also a commitment to accept the risk inherent in change.

At this point you may be asking yourself, are volunteers really worth all this? If volunteers aren't free labor, why do we want volunteers in the first place? You must look at your own organization to answer that question. Perhaps your organization is run completely by volunteers, in which case the question is easy to answer. Maybe your organization has a well established history of using volunteers to compliment your paid staff, for example, Boy Scouts. Maybe you think volunteers will be able to fill in the gaps which your paid staff cannot fill. Perhaps you want to increase community involvement through the use of volunteers, for example, public schools. Whatever the reason, understand in advance why you want volunteers as this will determine the direction of your program and the costs you are willing to underwrite.

It is easy to say you want to implement a volunteer program or increase the number of volunteers in an existing program. Actually doing it and doing it well, requires a plan, resources, and a steadfast commitment to make it work. You must understand why you want volunteers, what you want them to do, and how you can capitalize on their time and talent.

# 3

# WHAT DO YOU WANT VOLUNTEERS TO DO?

**Before you begin recruiting volunteers, decide exactly what you want them to do.** We need volunteers to help out around here is not enough to design a volunteer program and to begin recruiting volunteers. It might seem wise to get some volunteers, see what they can do, and then decide where you can use them. As logical as this may sound, it doesn't work in practice. First, look at your organization and find the opportunities to use volunteers.

If your organization already has volunteers, you have a base of experience and probably at least a few good volunteers. Find out what they are doing, exactly, not just helping with administration. The answer may be sorting and distributing incoming mail, making copies as required, and putting together new client packets using a checklist provided by the office manager. Ask existing volunteers what other jobs they think could be done by volunteers. Volunteers have surprising insight into organizations and where volunteers can be used.

**Ask supervisors what jobs they could use volunteers to do.** Include here, the nice to have work that may not have been done in the past. A clear understanding of what you want volunteers to do will help you find the people and talents you need. For example, if you are seeking volunteers to help in flood relief, distinguish between unskilled and skilled workers. Sand bag fillers are necessary at the height of the disaster. They need few specific skills, only the ability to work long hours. And you only need them for a few days. On the other hand, skilled workers, such as electricians and drywall hangers, who will be necessary later in the relief effort, will need specific skills and will be working for a longer period of time.

After getting the list of jobs, ask the supervisor to write a short job description for each job. This does not have to be long, but it does need to be specific.

### Example

The County Recreation Department needs volunteer softball coaches and staff. The department has prepared these job descriptions:

Team coach - Coaches youth softball team for girls ages 9-12 or boys ages 8-11. Teams have from 15 to 18 youths each. Teams practice two evenings per week for two hours and play games on Saturday mornings. Coaches are needed from first week of March through end of April. Love of children necessary. Knowledge of softball helpful. 12 coaches needed for each league.

Assistant coach - Assists youth softball team coach in coaching teams of girls ages 9-12 or boys ages 8-11. Teams have from 15 to 18 youths each. Teams practice two evenings per week for two hours and play games on Saturday mornings. Assistant coaches are needed from first week of March through end of April. Love of children necessary. Knowledge of softball not required. 24 assistant coaches needed for each league.

<u>League equipment manager</u> - Collects equipment from equipment issue, orders T-shirts and caps, and distributes these to team coaches at beginning of season. Collects equipment and returns it to the equipment issue section at end of season. Schedule is flexible from late February through first week of March and from last week in April through second week in May. One equipment manager needed per league.

Contrast these job descriptions with the following examples.

### Example

Friends of the Park needs volunteers to help build a mountain bike and equestrian trail at Fort Barkley State Park. Trail will eventually have 30 to 40 miles of trails.

County Rape Crisis Center needs volunteers to provide advocacy and support to victims reporting to County General Hospital.

In the County Recreation Department examples, the big job of operating the youth softball program has been divided into smaller jobs and each job description explains what the volunteer will be doing. In the latter two examples there appears to have been little forethought as to exactly what the volunteers will be doing. In the Friends of the Park example, a potential volunteer is likely to be scared away. What do they want, Paul Bunyon swinging his ax through the wilderness for 30 miles? In the County Rape Crisis Center example, are they looking for lawyers and social workers or was this a nice sounding phrase lifted directly out of their organizational purpose statement and made into a job description?

**Take the time to divide the work into smaller parts and write simple, accurate job descriptions.** These should include

**1)** a job title,

**2)** brief description of the work to be performed,

**3)** time required,

**4)** when the job must be performed, and

**5)** an estimate of the number of volunteers needed for this task. If two people can share one volunteer job, include this in the job description. The description should allow both the person recruiting volunteers and potential volunteers to get a quick grasp of what the job entails and when it can be done. Articulating specifics helps people considering volunteering decide whether this is a job they will be comfortable doing. It also lets the person recruiting volunteers see where he stands as he signs up volunteers and what jobs he needs to work harder to fill.

A few hours spent establishing exactly what you want your volunteers to do will save time throughout the volunteer program. It makes targeting groups and individuals for potential recruiting easier. When paid workers see exactly what volunteers will be doing, they are less likely to feel their own jobs are threatened and more likely to support the volunteer program. Additional supplies and equipment can be programmed in advance of the volunteers' actual arrival. Necessary training and forms can be developed in advance. In short, a clear focus on the volunteers' tasks makes the actual development or expansion of your existing program easier. Don't skip the job description step!

# 4

# RECRUITING VOLUNTEERS

Good volunteers will seldom beat a path to your door on their own. Just as trophy bass will not jump into the live well of your boat of their own accord, you have to fish for them. Successful fishermen will tell you that to catch fish you have to know what kind of fish you want to catch, where and when to fish for them, what bait to use, and how to land them.

**Knowing exactly what you are fishing for or what you want volunteers to do is the first step of recruiting.** Refer to your job descriptions. This will help you target potential volunteers. Do they have to be adults or can teens or younger children do the job? Do they need experience in a specific field or can you teach them the job? Do you want them to work with children, adults, animals, etc.? Is this a one day job or a job that recurs each week or month? Will the job require physical agility or can it be done from a sitting position? Does the job require face to face contact with people or can it be done over the phone? Narrow your focus on whom you are fishing for based on what you want them to do. Avoid the tendency to limit your focus to only your ideal volunteer. This way you will not inadvertently screen out potentially outstanding volunteers because they don't fit your ideal mold.

### Example

The Family Crisis Hotline needed volunteers to man their telephone hotlines. Although they placed a restriction on age, requiring volunteers to be 21 or older, they had few other restrictions. As a result they found Darlene, who has excellent interpersonal skills on the telephone and a real knack for listening and helping callers formulate plans for solving their problems. She soon became an invaluable part of their program. Darlene happens to be blind.

Identify the abilities you are seeking in volunteers, rather than concentrating on what people cannot do. Build on people's strengths for these strengths will enhance your volunteer program.

**Be prepared to explain in detail what you want prospective volunteers to do before you begin recruiting them.** Written job descriptions will make this easier. If you don't have job descriptions in writing, at least be certain you can articulate them on short notice as you begin the recruiting process. While you may wish to address all the volunteer opportunities your organization has, spend most of you effort recruiting for easy entry level jobs. Volunteers for your more involved or time consuming tasks are most likely to be recruited from volunteers already involved and experienced in your program. Make volunteering seem easy, which it will be if you concentrate on easy entry level jobs.

### Example

Meals on Wheels needs volunteers to deliver meals in a large metropolitan city.

If this is the only description of what volunteers will do, many good potential volunteers will never call. The potential volunteer sees herself with a carload of food carry out trays, struggling with a map to find addresses, and driving into unfamiliar and possibly dangerous areas of the city alone to deliver meals to total strangers. This is not an accurate description of what a new Meals on Wheels volunteer will do in a good program. However in the absence of information, it is only human nature to fill in the blanks with the worst possible scenario. It takes only a little more time to say that volunteers with transportation are needed to assist in the delivery of meals to homebound senior citizens in the city. Initially volunteers will accompany experienced volunteers to learn the routes and to meet the clients. Wherever possible, routes will be arranged as close to your home or work as feasible. Flexible schedules of days and times are available. Such a description lets the prospective volunteer know up front what she will be doing, for whom, and how much help and support she can expect.

**Make the job seem do-able by using an accurate job description.** If you are not specific, prospective volunteers may feel overwhelmed by the magnitude and difficulties of your volunteer opportunities and consequently decide not to volunteer. No matter how desperately you need someone to do an involved job, resist the urge to recruit a new volunteer to do it. First, you are unlikely to get a new volunteer with the knowledge and background you need. Second, the risk of failure to both your program and to the volunteer is too great.

### Example

Friends of the Library conducts an annual used book sale. The volunteer who had organized this sale for the past ten years has moved. Although all recognize that it must be done, no one in the organization wants to take on the job. In response to a general call for new Friends of the Library volunteers, Barbara offers to volunteer. She says she has management experience and has been the assistant manager of a bookstore. It would seem the prayers of Friends of the Library have been answered and Barbara is given the job of coordinating the book sale. She starts out with high energy and lots of enthusiasm, but as the weeks go by she is less and less visible. She fails to return phone calls. Soon the date for the book sale is only two weeks away and the books are still largely in boxes, unsorted, and stacked in the storeroom. An experienced, although reluctant, volunteer is then required to attempt to salvage the book sale resulting in long nights of work with other harried and unhappy volunteers. Barbara appears to be the villain in this example. In fact, the fault lies with the organization or Volunteer Coordinator, who gave her a job too difficult for a new volunteer. In addition to having a last minute crash to prepare for the book sale, Friends of the Library also lost a potentially fine volunteer in Barbara, who, having lost face, is unlikely to return.

**Don't give big jobs to new volunteers.** Advertise and recruit only for entry-level jobs to maximize your chances of getting and keeping good volunteers.

Some volunteer positions are for one time events. Examples include neighborhood or school clean up campaigns, food concessions at a festival day, visiting a nursing home on Grandparents' Day, painting the community center, etc. While the total number of volunteers needed for these events is usually large, the low commitment of volunteer time, usually just a few hours, makes recruiting for these easier. Target existing groups, such as civic organizations, youth clubs, and special interest groups. These groups may or may not have a goal related to your program. Don't limit yourself if you think you might be able to interest them in your program.

### Example

Save the Turtles is a volunteer program on the coast which monitors beaches where sea turtles nest and lay their eggs. Save the Turtles works to prevent damage to the nests and the newly hatched turtles. During nesting season, they need many volunteers to patrol the beaches where the turtles nest to ensure the safety of the turtles and their eggs. They request volunteers from the local Sierra Club, high school ecology groups, Explorer Scouts, garden clubs, service organizations, and local churches. Save the Turtles provides schedules for sign up and has experienced members of their group who give orientations on what to look for and who to notify of problems, as well as on site supervisors for each shift.

In seeking volunteers for one time, relatively simple tasks, recruiting groups has a much higher pay off than trying to recruit individuals. Networking with these groups, even those who turn you down, by asking if they know anyone else who might be interested in volunteering for your program will bring you greater exposure and ultimately more volunteers.

**If you want to catch fish, you've got to go fishing.** When you are recruiting volunteers you've got to tell people about your program and the opportunities you offer for volunteers. Advertising is valuable, especially if you can get pictures of people actually doing what you want volunteers to do. Pictures of people working at last month's event, for example, are great. Local newspapers will often run these information articles at no charge, particularly if they include pictures and names of people who live in their circulation area. Some newspapers even have regular space devoted to volunteer opportunities. Networking at your newspaper can pay off and may save you the expense of paid advertising, as shown in the following example of a weekly newspaper volunteer opportunities column.

### Example

Volunteer Opportunities

• Gulf Breeze residence for the elderly needs a volunteer with a car to pick up food orders at Food Source and bring them to the residence from 10:00 a.m. to noon on Fridays.
• The Compass and Connections mentor program of City Volunteers will train people interested in being role models for teens living in foster care. Training is Tuesday and Wednesday evening at the City Volunteer office.
• The Salvation Army Northside Branch in Centerville needs child-care assistants at least 18 years old from 7:00 a.m. to 6:00 p.m. in three-hour shifts weekdays.
• Memorial Hospital will host a "Bring a Buddy" brunch for prospective volunteers at 10:00 a.m. Monday in Hammel Auditorium behind the hospital
For more information on these and other volunteer opportunities, call City Volunteers at **222-5555**.

Think about where you would look for information if you were considering volunteering. Sometimes the classified ads can do double duty for you.

### Example: Double duty ads

Under the classification for Dogs:

---

Shetland Sheepdog Rescue has adult shelties available for adoption. Volunteers and foster homes needed. Call 111-9999.

**Advertising can be expensive.** Even if you can afford it, advertising is no substitute for talking to people. As a volunteer recruiter you are in fact a salesman selling your volunteer opportunities. If your program has a continuing need for volunteers, rather than one day events, you must talk to people you think are good volunteer candidates wherever you meet them. Start by interesting them in what you organization does. Contrary to popular opinion, people do care. You just have to hook them into caring about your program. Talk about what your organization does and who or what it helps. Don't try to get them to commit to volunteering immediately. Unless people really believe in your program and what you do, people have other things to do with their time. If you push them for a commitment, too often the response will be, "Are you kidding? I already have too much to do as it is without volunteering." Give people a chance to catch your enthusiasm for what you do. Share success stories with them. Invite them to just come by and see what you do. This is the classic no obligation, free trial. If they appear interested, drop the idea that you are always looking for good volunteers and that they don't have to make a long term commitment, just come try it out.

Despite your best efforts some people you think would make good volunteers will still tell you they aren't interested, they don't have time, or they will get back with you. Ask them if they know others who might be interested in volunteering with your organization. This expands your potential volunteer contacts and also allows the person a graceful way out of the conversation. Finally, give the person your organization's business card and phone number in case their schedule changes or they think of someone who might be interested.

**Recruiting volunteers can seem a lonely task, the exclusive domain of volunteer leaders and management.** In reality, your experienced volunteers, regardless of their job, can be your best recruiters. If they enjoy the program and what they are doing, they tell their friends. It may seem obvious — if they tell their friends, their friends will also volunteer. In reality, one does not necessarily follow the other. Volunteers don't automatically think about recruiting their friends. Therefore it is necessary to actively enlist your volunteers in the recruiting effort. Let them know you are always looking for new volunteers and the kinds of volunteer opportunities available, particularly if there are a variety of jobs and time periods to volunteer. Give your volunteers business cards for your organization and ask them to help you recruit people. Involving your current volunteers in recruiting lets them know their contributions and judgement are valuable. In the eyes of volunteers their status is elevated. After all, they must be good if management trusts them to look for new volunteers.

**Once people tell you they are interested, make it easy for them to volunteer.** Call, don't write! Your initial response to people who offer to volunteer is crucial. Exact words are less important than an attitude of enthusiasm and delight that this person has offered to volunteer with your program. After all, he is offering to give you his time and abilities. Talk briefly about your program and your volunteer opportunities. Then listen to what he is interested in doing and the time he has available. Be prepared to invite him to a volunteer opportunity on a specific day. If this is not possible, tell him of future events and that someone will call him a week or so before the event to invite him to come. The person who makes the first call doesn't have to be the one who makes the follow up call. But be certain that someone does follow up and that they, too, are enthusiastic about your program and this new volunteer's potential involvement. In short, let people know you are glad they have offered to volunteer and you want them to be a part of the team.

Promptness in making calls to people who have indicated an interest in volunteering cannot be over emphasized. If you don't call them quickly, good volunteers will find another organization to volunteer with. Others will simply lose interest. It takes considerable initiative and a certain degree of courage for a person to call an organization to volunteer in the first place. Not receiving a prompt positive reception can not only turn them off to your program, but possibly to other volunteer efforts as well. No matter how many prospective volunteers you have talked to, remember you may be the first person from your organization the caller has talked to. First impressions set the tone.

### Example

Hi, Carol. This is Charlayne Porter from the Civic Center. I understand you are interested in volunteering at the Civic Center and I'm so pleased you called. We need new volunteers, especially to usher at major events. We also have a few other volunteer opportunities. Do you have an particular interests?

. . . . Well, ushering is where people usually start out. What we will do is schedule you initially for a smaller event to help you get oriented. I will pair you with an experienced volunteer, who will show you what to do the first time. Are there any days or times that are especially good or bad for you?

. . . . We have a chamber orchestra concert in two weeks, Thursday evening the 23rd. Would that fit your schedule?

. . . . Great! Margaret Grenville is working with new volunteers that night and she will give you a call. If you don't hear from her or have questions in the meantime, please call me at 555-3333. I'm so glad you called us and I'm looking forward to meeting you in person soon.

Let your well organized program and existing volunteers sell your program to new volunteers. Get new volunteers in the door first by getting them to bite with your enthusiasm and what your program has to offer, showing them they can make a difference, and then setting the hook by giving them an easy entry level job to start.

### Recruiting volunteers is a continuous process.
Attrition is a fact of life in volunteer programs. Even the most dedicated volunteers, not to mention the less committed, leave because they move, experience changes in their family situation, change jobs, have health problems, etc. This is not all bad. Adding new volunteers actually improves programs by adding new talent, fresh ideas, and energy. No volunteer program is so secure that it does not need at least a trickle of new volunteers all the time.

# 5

# WHY VOLUNTEERS SIGN UP (AND WHY THEY DON'T)

Nearly everyone who works with volunteers has also been a volunteer in the past. It's worth recalling your own experience the first time you signed up to volunteer. You know why you volunteered. Remember, though, you are unique. Not everyone thinks the way you do and you may find some of the reasons people give surprising, especially for why people decide not to sign up to volunteer. First let's look at the reasons people give for signing up to volunteer.

➤ **They care about your cause or the people you serve.** People who feel strongly committed to the people or the cause your program supports, for example, neighborhood crime watch, will always be the core of your program. They believe in what you are doing and they are ready to help by volunteering their time and abilities. To keep these volunteers it is essential that from the very beginning, they feel what they are doing as a volunteer is actually making a difference. These volunteers must be able to see a direct link between what they are doing and the cause or the people you serve.

➤ **They want to make a difference.** These are volunteers who feel a strong social commitment to give of themselves to make a difference for others. They want to be part of the action. This desire to make a difference is somewhat mercurial in that if the volunteer program does not snap them up and promptly give them a job to do, their enthusiasm for your program quickly cools and they move on to something else. To keep these volunteers, like those who care (and often they are one in the same), they must be able to see the results of what they are doing both in the short and long term. When a volunteer program has established measurable goals and can show results, these volunteers know their contributions matter. For example, a church volunteer program to visit shut-ins increased the total number of shut-ins visited regularly from 64 to 85 last year and increased the number of visits from an average of one visit a month to an average of 1.8 visits per month. This kind of data lets potential volunteers see how their volunteering can make a difference.

### ➤ It's a skill they do well or are interested in.

Volunteers do best and participate more in things they enjoy. People who enjoy music, for example, are more likely to volunteer for programs involving music. This appears obvious. It is, unfortunately, often overlooked in recruiting volunteers. When you need volunteers to do a particular job, find and target first people who already have an interest in and enjoy this kind of work. If you want volunteers for a community garden program, for example, reach out to garden clubs and to people that networking tells you are talented gardeners. Recognizing their expertise is often a way to get them involved.

### ➤ They have friends who volunteer with the program.

These people already know a lot about the program and the volunteers you already have. They also know that someone whose judgement they trust likes volunteering with the program. Encouraging volunteers to bring their friends or family members to volunteer has excellent potential for success. It brings you volunteers who know what they are getting into. The only possible problem with this is that you may end up with cliques of friends who do not wish to work with others. Anticipate this in advance and don't allow these groups of friends to become too entrenched. Start early to gradually move them to different areas and responsibilities.

➤ **They are seeking more fulfillment and challenge than their job offers.** Many people find their regular jobs professionally and financially rewarding, but not personally fulfilling. They may be in a job that limits their contact with people. Or they may want to develop skills which their job does not allow them to do. Their regular job may not give them the appreciation or sense of achievement they seek. Volunteering gives them the fulfillment they are looking for. It is not unusual for people to tell you they enjoy their volunteer job more than their paid job. Often these are people with exceptional talents. To keep them volunteering, though, you must quickly incorporate them into your program and give them an opportunity to work in an area in which they are interested.

➤ **They want to meet people and make friends. In our society many people are lonely or seeking social contact.** People who have experienced major changes in their lives, such as death, divorce, children leaving home, or moving to a new community are often drawn to volunteer programs. Besides being able to contribute, these volunteers need to be introduced to and work with other volunteers. They are not good candidates for support jobs that limit their contact with people. Just because they want to make friends, does not automatically mean they are outgoing and the ideal candidates to be your up front meet and greet volunteers. Get to know these volunteers as individuals and ensure they are working with other volunteers with whom they have things in common and can identify. Helping them to become part of a small team will increase their confidence. When your program meets their need for friends, they are likely to continue volunteering.

> **There is something in it for them**. Parents who volunteer to be scout troop leaders in order for their child to be in scouts are classic examples of this motivation. There are also people who wish to be seen volunteering with an organization primarily because it can advance them socially or on the job. Volunteering with a community service program can be an effective means of being recognized and then invited to join a selective club or service organization. An organization to which they already belong may require them to volunteer. Some organizations, such as the Junior League and the Jaycees, require their members to volunteer a certain number of hours in the community. Just because these volunteers have secondary motives does not mean they won't make excellent volunteers. They are often very talented and superb performers. However, it is important to remember they are oriented on their goal. The jobs you ask them to do must further that goal or they will be unlikely to continue volunteering with your program.

> **The boss says volunteer.** This may sound like a contradiction. How can this person really be a volunteer? Particularly if the boss is giving the volunteer paid time away from work to volunteer, this type of volunteer can be both reliable and dedicated provided they and their boss get the appropriate feedback. In addition to giving the volunteer a meaningful job and letting her know you value her work, you must also get that message through to her boss.

# ...AND WHY THEY DON'T

Although these are the most common reasons for signing up to volunteer, they are certainly not all inclusive. The reasons people give for not signing up to volunteer are less obvious, but worth understanding if you wish to increase your volunteer base.

➤ **I don't have enough time.** Of all the reasons people give for not volunteering, this one comes up most often. The fact is everyone has the same amount of time in their day, 24 hours. It is what people choose to do with their time that differs. People find time to do the things they enjoy, which can include volunteering. Busy people often make some of the best volunteers because they know how to organize their time and get things done. When a potential volunteer says he doesn't have time, it may mean just that. It may also be a subtle way of saying he isn't interested in giving time to your program. The challenge here is to present your program as something he will enjoy doing and that may compliment one of his interests. People make time for the things they enjoy.

## Example

Max is a busy executive in a new job. His interests are hiking and the out outdoors. He has been a good volunteer in the past, but says he doesn't have enough time now to volunteer, especially since he feels he should be spending more time with his daughter who is 11. If a volunteer opportunity were presented to Max in such a way that it would allow him to spend more time with his daughter and more time in the outdoors, he would jump at the chance.

When people tell you they don't have time to volunteer,

listen to what they would like to do if they had more time. If your program can fit what they would like to do and if you can assure them the initial time obligation will not be excessive, you can bring them into your program at least for a sample.

**➤ They may have a preconceived idea about your program from current or former volunteers and some of this publicity may not be positive.** Make sure the person has the correct information about how you currently operate, what your program does, and the volunteer opportunities you offer. It's also useful here to invite them to come see what your volunteers do without having to make a commitment to work. For example, invite them to come by your Habitat for Humanity building site to see what you are doing. Recognizing and greeting them when they come by will go a long way toward making them feel wanted. If they are still not interested, give them an opportunity to save face by asking if they know anyone else who might be interested. Also, tell them that if their situation changes, you would like to have them as a volunteer and give them your card so they can easily call you.

**➤ They don't want to make a big time commitment.** Especially when people are not exactly sure what they are getting into with a volunteer program, they are reluctant to commit to volunteering their time. This occurs most often with people who have volunteered before and have had a bad experience. Frequently these are busy people with skills you could use. Make it easy for them to volunteer and don't ask for a big up front commitment of time. People will be glad to give you their time if they enjoy what they are doing. First, though, they must feel comfortable they know what they are getting into and exactly how much time it will take. Vague or indefinite descriptions, such as, we work until the job is done, are red flags to these people. Instead, offer them a sample, a short specific amount of time on an easy day of their choice, if possible. For example, no matter how badly you need to get volunteers to work the annual rummage sale, you may have difficulty finding volunteers if you don't break the work down into smaller pieces. Ask people to spend two hours one Saturday morning sorting contributions. A two hour commitment is acceptable. Then if the person enjoys what she is doing, she will be more likely to give additional time and take on a greater commitment.

### ➤ They can't come when you need them.
Sometimes the people you would like to have volunteer aren't available when you need them. Wherever possible look at ways to modify your program to permit maximum flexibility in work hours. Perhaps you can use the volunteer to do another job that needs doing, but not at your regular Wednesday morning time. For example, the volunteer might be able to mail out information to clients or assist paid workers in another facet of your program on another day. Allowing people to job share has the same advantages with volunteer programs as it has in business. It increases your workforce by permitting two people to split the work. For example, if you are having difficulty finding volunteers to staff the reception desk in a hospital on Friday evenings, consider asking two volunteers to share the job with each working only every other Friday. If you truly want volunteers, you must seek ways to make volunteering convenient for their schedules.

### ➤ They are afraid.
You will almost never be told this directly; however, fear is an underlying reason in many cases when people decide not to volunteer. They are afraid they will make mistakes, be embarrassed, or will be unable

to do the work. They are afraid people won't talk to them or they won't have any friends in the volunteer program. Fear is a powerful motivator. For those who lead or work in volunteer programs, this can be hard to believe. After all, you are nice people. You will teach them everything they need to know. They will enjoy volunteering, if they will just give it a chance. These points are all true, but a potential volunteer does not know you and your program like you do. The trick with people who are afraid is to introduce them to your program gently. This may mean giving them the opportunity to hear or read letters from satisfied clients of your program. It nearly always means bringing them to your program and showing them what you do and how they can help. Sometimes it means temporarily bringing the program to them.

### Example

Butler Elementary School needs volunteer grandparents to work with and encourage students who are having difficulty in reading and basic arithmetic. The program coordinator for the school approached the activities director of a retirement community. Flyers asking for volunteers produced little interest in the community. The program coordinator recognized one of the problems. The school was in a poor neighborhood, unlike where most of the retirees had lived. She arranged to take ten of the children to the retirement community to read to the retirees. All of the children had reading difficulties, but they gave it their best effort. Two of the retirees, who had been asked in advance to do this, invited individual children to sit with them and read. Soon every child had one or more retirees listening and helping them. The whole program took less than 45 minutes. Before leaving, the program coordinator and the activities director offered the retirees the opportunity to go to the school one afternoon a week to help children read. The retirement community provided transportation and the school paired children who needed help with individual retiree volunteers. The program grew and thrived as volunteers began telling their friends how much they enjoyed the program and the children.

**Although fear may be more common with older volunteers, it is not exclusive to any age group.** Adolescents, who can be exceptional volunteers, are often terrified at the thought of doing something outside the mainstream. Besides the fear of being embarrassed by perhaps not knowing what to do, they are afraid of being out of place and having no friends. When fear is a factor in deciding not to volunteer, the best way to overcome it is to recruit these people in groups of two or more. If they try volunteering with a friend, they are more likely to feel comfortable and to be interested in returning, especially if they start out with an easy nonthreatening job and a short initial time commitment. Although they may be timid in the beginning, these people can become some of your most valuable volunteers if introduced to your program correctly.

Insight into the reasons people do and do not sign up to volunteer, will make it easier to design your recruiting efforts. It also illustrates why volunteers' first experience with your program is so important. If you don't make volunteering easy and the first experience enjoyable, volunteers won't come back.

# 6

# MAKE IT EASY TO VOLUNTEER

Once you have determined why you want volunteers, what you want them to do, and have begun recruiting, you must make it easy for people to volunteer. Let people know you are looking for volunteers. Tell your paid staff, existing volunteers, and local community volunteer coordinators. Check with your United Way. Advertise by placing flyers where you think you will reach prospective volunteers. Examples include grocery store bulletin boards, hospital and doctor's office waiting rooms (especially if you are seeking retired and senior volunteers), and school cafeteria bulletin boards if you are seeking student volunteers. People are most likely to read your flyer where they are having to wait or stand in line.

**Be more than a telephone number.** Twenty-four hour voice mail is fine. Just be sure the people who call your voice mail get a prompt call back by a person knowledgeable about volunteer opportunities. Nothing is more frustrating to a potential volunteer as no return call or an answer from someone who knows little about the volunteer program.

### Example

Rich has been a competitive distance runner since high school. He recently moved to a large city on the West Coast. Seeing an ad for an upcoming charity run, Rich called to offer his help as a volunteer, thinking this might be a good way to get to know people in his new city. Rich called the agency conducting the run and described his previous experience.

Rich: Do you need volunteers to help with the run?

Agency: Yes, we need lots of volunteers.

Rich: What do you need volunteers to do?

Agency: Well, I don't know exactly what you would be doing, but we really need volunteers.

Rich: If I leave you my name and phone number, would you have someone call me with the specifics of what you would like me to do:

(After two weeks passed with no call, Rich called again.)

Agency: Oh, yes, we still need volunteers. I don't know why no one called you.

Rich: How can I get more information?

Agency: Come on down to our office and someone can talk with you. We are in the City Center Building in downtown.

Rich: Where should I go when I get there?

Agency: Just come to the parking lot.

Rich: Are there designated parking spots for volunteers:

Agency: No, but it's not very expensive to park in our lot.

Needless to say, Rich did not pursue volunteer opportunities with this agency nor did he participate in their charity run.

**Know exactly what you want volunteers to do and be prepared to explain volunteer opportunities in the first call.** Volunteers are often hesitant and fear being embarrassed. Tell them exactly what you would like volunteers to do and when. If there are choices, now is the time to explain them and let the volunteer decide what he wishes to do.

### Example

Diane and Bob called a community soup kitchen to volunteer their help on Thanksgiving Day. The person who took their call told them volunteers were needed in two hour shifts beginning at 9:00 a.m. Volunteers were needed in three areas: preparation of food for serving, actual serving of food on the line, and clean up. He also told them they needed volunteers as floaters to do any job needed. Diane and Bob volunteered as floaters from 12:00 to 2:00 p.m. When they arrived, they were met and told that the kitchen was being over run by dirty pots and pans. Diane and Bob spent their time washing pots and pans and cleaning up the dining area. They felt good about their Thanksgiving volunteering and will volunteer again next year with the same program. Organization and knowing in advance what tasks needed to be done made this agency's use of volunteers a success.

**Invite new volunteers to help at a specific activity.** Give day, time, and location. Be prepared to give detailed instructions on how to find the facility and where to park. Poor directions can lose a volunteer before she even starts. Always assume the person volunteering is not familiar with your location until they tell you otherwise. Be prepared to give instructions for mass transit if you are in a metropolitan area.

### Example

Directions given by someone who has routinely driven to the facility many times may go something like this: "We're

---

off Millwood Avenue, a little past the mall. After you pass the mall you will see a road to the right. I don't know the name of it, but turn there and we will be on the left. You can't miss it."

In fact, you can miss it. It is useful to have written instructions near the telephone that clearly explain how to find your facility coming from different directions. This makes it easy for anyone giving directions to do a good job. Not every volunteer drives. In some cases it may be important to offer to have someone drive them to the facility and then drive them back home after they have finished volunteering. Transportation of volunteers can be another volunteer job. Tell prospective volunteers where to park and what entrance to use. If you are in a city or crowded area, have close in designated parking for volunteers. If possible, have someone expecting the new volunteer near the entrance to welcome them and show them where they will be working.

**Pair each new volunteer with an experienced volunteer.** Most organizations have a few outgoing volunteers who will enjoy this task. Expect new volunteers to be nervous and apprehensive. Having someone who has been in their shoes before show them the ropes will make their first volunteer experience smoother.

**Give volunteers a place to work, adequate equipment, and necessary supplies.** Depending on what you want them to do, this may mean a preprinted worksheet, a hammer, a table or desk, a chair, writing supplies, a telephone, or access to a computer. Be ready for them. Do not expect the volunteer to get out and set up supplies, or to have to ask for them. Standing around with your hands in your pockets waiting to be told what to do is not a fun volunteer experience.

### Example

Jennifer, an experienced paralegal, volunteered with the city legal aid society. She is the kind of person who can quickly solve many problems over the phone or through letters. She was never given a desk or access to a phone. Jennifer did not expect a dedicated desk and phone. She did expect the society to have a desk or table and phone designated for all volunteers to use. Her requests for a place to work were met with responses such as, "Yes, we know we need to set up a volunteer work space, but we just don't have a place right now." After a few weeks of working off a tablet on her lap and standing to borrow a paid staff member's phone, Jennifer stopped volunteering.

**Teach the new volunteer what you want her to do.** The volunteer partner may do this or if you have a large group of new volunteers you may wish to teach a short class. Do not expect the volunteer to figure it out on her own. A little coaching and encouragement at this stage will produce a confident volunteer and will prevent problems later. It is not necessary to conduct a formal six week course of instruction, for example, for volunteers before they can begin volunteering. Such a big advance time commitment can be a disincentive to volunteering at all.

### Example

Monica, a new volunteer with a pet adoption program, was asked to help at the registration table on adoption day. She was given application blanks and pens. Another volunteer told her to have people interested in adopting a cat or dog fill out the form, look at the animals, and list their preferences. At the end of the adoption, she was asked where she put the money. Only then was she told she should have been collecting an application fee.

**Arrange for volunteers to eat if their volunteer time goes over a normal meal.** This is especially important for new volunteers. It may mean bringing in food for volunteers or giving them a pass to allow them to eat in the agency or school cafeteria, possibly, but not necessarily, at no charge. More significantly, it means someone inviting the new volunteer to join them for the meal, even if there are no meals served on the premises. Eating a meal by yourself in new or strange surroundings will not enhance a new volunteer's feeling of belonging. Do not assume the volunteer will see others leaving for lunch and do likewise.

*Example*

Complimentary take-out meals had been provided by a fast food restaurant for instructors at a Red Cross safety training workshop. Classes had staggered starts which meant some ran over the lunch period. Instructor trainers were scheduled to relieve each volunteer instructor to allow the volunteer time to eat lunch. Scheduling instructor trainers to do this took time and coordination. It paid off, however, as volunteer instructors did a better job in the afternoon and continued to return as volunteers for future training sessions.

**Make it easy for people to volunteer from the start.** Ultimately, you may want volunteers to have more skills, more training, and more experience. These goals can wait. First you must get people to volunteer and to enjoy what they are doing. Keep the door open. Welcome them and give them a chance to contribute. Value their contributions and show volunteers that you appreciate their willingness to give you their time and talents by the way you treat them from the very beginning.

# 7

# ENTRY LEVEL JOBS

Businesses have entry level jobs for the same reason volunteer programs should have them. Entry level jobs reduce risk, both for the organization and for the volunteer. From the new volunteer's perspective an easy job in the beginning is less threatening. As they gain confidence, they can take on more challenging jobs. From management's point of view, if a volunteer makes a mistake in an easy entry level job, the cost to the organization is low. Correcting the error is easy to do. Entry level jobs also give management an opportunity to observe the volunteer and determine where he can best fit in the organization.

### *Example*

Vickie has volunteered to be a Girl Scout troop leader. Before committing her to a troop or sending her to their training programs, Vickie is first asked to be an understudy or assistant to an experienced troop leader. This allows her to get a feel for the job without risking embarrassment or mistakes. If she is comfortable after a few weeks and if the experienced troop leader feels she has the potential, then she will be sent to training and assigned a troop of her own.

In this example had Vickie been unreliable, often missing meetings or not completing projects she had undertaken, it would have been much better to learn this before she was given a regular troop leader position. It would also have saved management the expenditure of valuable training resources. Entry level jobs make these general observations of style easier to recognize and to deal with. From the volunteer's perspective, a lower risk entry level job gives her an opportunity to see how the organization operates and to decide whether she really wants to commit herself to volunteering on a regular basis.

Examples of entry level jobs include such tasks as playing cards and board games with hospital patients, assisting an experienced volunteer in shelving returned books at the library, working as a carpenter's helper, etc. In fact some volunteer opportunities are simply one time entry level jobs. These include painting over graffiti or picking up litter in a wildlife area. Whatever the task, it must be easy and it must not be done alone. Few experiences are as lonely or unrewarding as doing an unfamiliar task in a new setting by yourself. A supervisor who is committed to volunteers succeeding in the organization and who is comfortable working with new people can make or break a new volunteer's first experience.

**No job is self explanatory, regardless of how easy it may seem to management.** Even the most well intentioned and energetic new volunteers will make mistakes unless someone takes time to show them what to do and what standards are expected. If at all possible, show new volunteers, rather than tell them. A hands on approach builds confidence in the new volunteer who says to herself, "If you can do this, so can I." Showing also brings up the glitches or peculiarities in a task, such as a balky computer you routinely have to reboot or a dog that lunges on the leash. Patient coaching in the beginning on an entry level job will go far to boost a new volunteer's confidence and sense of satisfaction.

Some jobs which may seem like easy entry level jobs are neither easy nor basic. A classic example is answering the telephone. Unless all you want the volunteer to do is pick up the phone receiver and say, "Good morning, Family Counseling Services.", this is not an easy job. People who call your organization need more than a greeting. They will have questions about who they should speak to or when programs are being offered or whether your organization can help them. Not knowing the answers to questions is at best frustrating and at worst embarrassing. Telling a new volunteer to ask if he doesn't know the answer doesn't solve the problem. After a new volunteer has asked questions four or five times, he gets tired of this. It will take an exceptional volunteer to keep coming back if answering the phone is their first experience with your program.

**Some organizations require extensive up front training before new volunteers are ever allowed to volunteer.** Occasionally new volunteers are even required to join the organization and pay dues before they can receive this training. At first glance this practice might seem to make it easier for the volunteer when she actually has her first day of volunteering. From the organization's point of view, this way they can weed out those people who are not really serious. Unfortunately this practice also weeds out some excellent potential volunteers who are unwilling to commit up front time and money before they know exactly what they are getting into and whether the volunteer opportunity will give them the pay back they seek in personal satisfaction. This practice also sends the subtle message to volunteers that they are not good enough to volunteer without training. Organizations that require up front training often find themselves asking why they can't get enough volunteers. Often they conclude there just aren't enough people out there who care. This is not the case. They have just made it too hard to volunteer.

### Example

Frank is a college graduate with a degree in English. He recently retired from a successful career in business and contacted an adult literacy tutoring program to explore the possibility of volunteering. Frank has a flexible schedule and time to contribute. He is informed that before he can volunteer he must complete 20 hours of instruction and join the literacy organization, a fee of $25. The instruction will take place over a month and will require ten forty mile round trips to a neighboring community. Rather than expend this much time and money on a program he doesn't know, Frank declines. He contacts the public schools in his town and is quickly incorporated into a high school tutoring program for poor readers. After one week of understudying with an experienced volunteer tutor, Frank is soon volunteering three mornings a week as a reading tutor with this program.

From the adult literacy group's point of view, they had weeded Frank out as not really being serious. In fact they lost a superb volunteer by being inflexible and refusing to give him an entry level sample of their program. Training is desirable and often necessary if a volunteer is to move beyond an entry level job. First, though, it is imperative to get volunteers in the door and doing something in which they can take pride, a job in which they can contribute.

**Entry level jobs are not an end in themselves**, although some volunteers and some volunteer programs will use them in this way. Delivering emergency supplies to storm victims and painting the community center are examples of entry level jobs that are often one time volunteer opportunities. Wise volunteer programs, however, are always on the look out for individuals participating in these activities who have potential to do more with the organization. Don't assume these volunteers will return to participate in future volunteer programs, make it a point to invite them back. Get their phone numbers and call them to invite them to specific activities you think they would enjoy and could contribute to.

**Remember, an entry level job should be just that.** Giving a new volunteer a job that is too big or too difficult can run him off. Even though the job can be done by one experienced volunteer, don't saddle a new volunteer with a hard job. The purpose of entry level jobs is to get volunteers to come back and to continue volunteering.

Some new volunteers will be comfortable with the entry level job and will be happy to do it indefinitely. However, most volunteers will soon seek more challenging work. The Volunteer Coordinator must be sensitive to the comfort level of volunteers, but still offer them new jobs to do. As a general rule, several days at an entry level job should give the supervisor or Volunteer Coordinator enough insight into the new volunteer's strengths to offer them a more advanced job.

When a volunteer's first experience with your organization is positive, she is likely to return. Make sure she returns by the way you acknowledge her contributions from day one. She is giving you her time and talents. She does not have to do this. A sincere thank you can make the difference.

# 8

# LEADING VOLUNTEERS

Volunteers are harder to lead than paid employees. Unlike paid workers, volunteers get no paycheck and have no binding contract. You have no power or authority over volunteers except what they give you. Volunteers work for you because they enjoy what they do. They feel their work makes a difference and is appreciated. Only positive leadership is effective with volunteers. Threaten or verbally abuse a volunteer and he will leave. The volunteer loses nothing except aggravation. You, however, lose a volunteer worker.

To be successful volunteers have to be led with the carrot rather than the stick. This is not a new concept, however it may be foreign to some who lead volunteers. When your experience has been in authoritarian or parental supervision, such as that often used with children and in some lines of work where employees have little choice but to obey, this may require changes to your leadership style. "You have to do it because I say so." doesn't work with volunteers. Like it or not, they don't have to do it.

Volunteers expect to be respected as individuals with good sense, even children who volunteer. They expect to be asked, rather than told to do things and they also expect at least a short explanation of why.

### Example
Karen, a high school senior, has volunteered for Habitat

---

for Humanity for several years and is now a crew leader. On this particular day, she is supervising the laying of tile in the kitchen and bathroom of a new house. Ron, a new volunteer in his thirties, has been assigned to Karen's crew. He begins telling Karen and the other workers how to more quickly do the job. Karen tells him that she knows what she is doing and if he is not comfortable with this, he should talk to her supervisor, Dave. Ron takes his problem to Dave. Rather than immediately moving Ron to another crew, Dave takes time to explain that despite her age, Karen is experienced and is doing the task correctly. The technique Ron was proposing would prevent good adhesion of the tiles. Dave tells Ron he needs him on the tile crew, however, he will move him to another crew if Ron prefers. Because he was asked and because Dave took the time to explain the reasons to him, Ron stayed with the tile crew.

If this seems you have to spoon feed or coddle volunteers, in a sense you do. Especially in the beginning, you are courting volunteers so they will want to give their time and abilities to your program. Everyone wants to be somebody special. Volunteer supervisors can make people feel special by the manner in which they lead them.

In paid jobs, if you are the boss, you generally have the right to determine exactly how a job will be done (unless your boss takes that prerogative away and tells you how to do it). Good leaders know that getting worker input before deciding on a plan almost always produces a better plan and in every case gets workers more involved and committed to the final outcome. This is especially true with volunteers. Taking time to listen to their ideas, even if not all of them are workable, is important. Volunteers are willingly giving their time. They also want to give their ideas and to have those ideas respected and considered.

**Leaders who cannot accept input from their workers or who must personally control every step of the process will be very frustrated working with volunteers.** Except for the few volunteers who are easily intimidated by authority figures, high control does not work with volunteers. The volunteer will say, "I don't need this. I'm out of here." Similarly keeping the majority of the volunteers in the worker bee role, with only a select few controlling all decisions and plans will result in volunteer attrition over time.

The shortest distance between two points is a straight line. However, that may not be the best route when you use volunteers. If the volunteer is willing to do the work and her style does not seriously conflict with organization policies, accept the fact that the work may not be done in the most efficient manner. The end justifies the means: keep the volunteer and let her work at her pace and in her style.

**Sometimes, though, the volunteer's style makes other peoples' work more difficult or clashes with organization policies.** In these cases, coaching volunteers to improved performance can be a challenge. For some leaders coaching comes naturally. For others it requires a change in their style. Telling volunteers directly how to improve their performance can be quick! It can also cause volunteers to lose face and leave. A more effective approach is to praise what they are doing right, ask the volunteer how he thinks his work could be improved, and then make suggestions on how you think he might do his job better or more easily. Explain the negative impact his style is having on other volunteers or the program. He may need training, so be prepared to listen and be willing to get him the help or training he needs. Presenting improvement in a positive, rather than a critical manner and involving the volunteer and his ideas in the discussion take more time. In the long run, though, it will produce better results.

**Volunteers are human.** They want to do a good job and they thrive on support and praise. Beyond holding the carrot out front, leaders must occasionally give them a carrot or two to eat. Praise them for their achievements and contributions. This goes for experienced as well as new volunteers. Don't wait to put it in a letter! Speak out with sincerity, every day you work with volunteers. Find something to praise. Even when you feel totally frustrated, a few words of praise to a volunteer will not only make her feel good, it will also help your mood. Effective volunteer leaders do not dwell on the negative.

Unfortunately, in the rush of trying to get things done, new volunteers may get the praise while long time volunteers have become such a part of the program they get taken for granted and receive little or no feedback other than at the annual thank you event. Long time volunteers tend to be given a job, which they do well, and then left on their own to do it. A few hardy souls may tolerate this and continue to volunteer. The majority, however, will drift away from you program. You may even find some of them spending more time volunteering for other programs where they feel their efforts are appreciated.

Besides praising their good work, feedback to experienced volunteers should include asking them for suggestion on improving or expanding the program. They are a gold mine of information, if you will only ask them. Give experienced volunteers the opportunity to become supervisors or to move into other more responsible positions. Offering them additional training at a more advanced level is another way to recognize their contributions. This training, if at all possible, should be funded by the organization, not the volunteer. You have a considerable investment in your experienced volunteers and replacing them is not easy. Make sure they know you appreciate them.

## Support for volunteers takes many forms.

Although you don't pay volunteers for their work, they cannot be expected to do everything with nothing. In some situations you know the support volunteers need, such as getting their computer terminal repaired or getting more workers for the job. Visit the volunteer work site while volunteers are working to see what support might be needed. Ask volunteers if there are things they need to do their job better. If you ask, they will tell you. They will also appreciate being asked.

Asking questions about support may seem like looking for trouble. It is instead an important facet of leading volunteers which helps volunteer retention. A volunteer who is not getting the support he needs, may or may not ask his supervisor for help. If the supervisor has never asked him what he needs, he may assume no one cares or that he wouldn't get it anyway. In some cases this is true, but more often if the supervisor knew he needed something and could get it for him, the supervisor would get it. Ask the question. When volunteers perceive they are not getting the support they need, they leave. These volunteers may never tell the leader that lack of support is the reason they are leaving. Sometimes the support can be simple and surprisingly cheap.

### *Example: LIsten to the voice of experience!*

The First Church had a large congregation and had used volunteers for some time to direct parking in and out of the parking lot for church services. The church was on a busy street and volunteers in church clothes could not easily be seen, so the church had safety vests for the volunteers. These worked well, but recently there had been several incidents of volunteers being nearly hit by cars in the parking lot when drivers were not paying attention. An experienced volunteer suggested each volunteer be given a whistle to get drivers' attention in these cases. Not only did the whistles improve safety, they gave the volunteers another kind of recognition or status symbol with little cost to the church.

**Plan for more volunteers than you think you will need.** In business, if you think the job will take six workers, you assign six workers. (In today's downsizing climate, you may only be able to assign four workers.) However, with volunteers you must "over resource." If the job needs six workers you would be wise to schedule nine volunteers to do the job. This is not because volunteers are inept. Rather it is because you must expect no-shows. Like it or not, it is a fact that volunteers often feel less responsibility for being where they say they will be and on time than paid employees. Leaders can be frustrated by this when they need six workers and only four show up. Such frustration is a frequent cause of leaders leaving volunteer programs. Expect fewer people to show up than you have asked for and counter this tendency by asking for more workers than you think you will need. How many more depends on your particular situation. A general rule of thumb, though, is probably 30% more than you actually need. Over resource your work to reduce frustration with no-shows.

---

Occasionally over resourcing work can result in more people showing up than are actually needed. At these times volunteer leaders must be able to think on their feet and redistribute the work, adjust the schedule, or add new work to the job to keep all the volunteers involved. Be careful, though, to avoid the trap of make work jobs that make volunteers feel their presence is not valued. It is far better to do the job and finish early than to keep everyone busy for the full amount of time scheduled. Let's face it — everyone enjoys the unexpected freedom of getting off from work early. Volunteers are no exception.

Some volunteers are exceptionally reliable and are an exception to the no-show phenomenon. These volunteers not only come every time they are scheduled, they regularly put in more hours than they are scheduled for and willingly take on more work. Don't expect or make them take up the slack for no-shows on a regular basis. Actively recruit more volunteers or reduce the scope of the program so that this hard core of volunteers is not overworked. If you overload these conscientious volunteers, sooner or later they will feel they are being taken advantage of. By the time this happens, it is difficult to change the pattern and these stalwart volunteers will become disillusioned and bitter and quit.

**Flexibility is critical to success as a volunteer leader.** The structure that exists in business does not automatically exist in volunteer programs. Unlike business, volunteers rather than leaders determine how much structure there will be. Volunteers decide whether they will work, when they will work, and how hard they will work. This is an over simplification, but the bottom line is that volunteers control their work, not the bosses. Leaders must therefore be willing to adjust their program to fit their volunteers.

### Example

Live Oak School actively recruited volunteer tutors for its students. They received a number of calls from people who wanted to volunteer but could not come during the school day. Tutoring was extended to the after school program which incorporated a few of these volunteers. However, there were others who worked until 5:30 p.m. and still could not participate. Using flexibility, the principal began a program of after school homework tutoring using the telephone. Students with homework questions could call a voice mail number between 6:00 and 8:30 p.m. and leave their name, grade, telephone number, and subject they were having difficulty with. Volunteer tutors were scheduled to check the voice mail and then assist students over the phone that same evening. This expanded tutoring program allowed not only their original volunteers who could not come during the school day to participate, it also opened opportunities for volunteers with physical disabilities who were un able to come to the school.

In addition to creative thinking and planning, flexibility often requires additional resources. In this situation, it required the installation of a voice mail phone number, scheduling of volunteers, and training of volunteers to handle homework questions. Obviously some screening was needed of volunteers in this expanded program to rule out those who might abuse this contact with children. Additionally parental support had to be developed. Being flexible is not always easy. It is, however, often the difference between outstanding and mediocre volunteer programs.

Another aspect of flexibility is being able to work with what you have. This applies to the people who volunteer as well as to facilities. Volunteer programs are not a perfect world. You can ask for and recruit for the skills and the numbers you want, however, it is rare to get exactly what you want when you want it. This can be discouraging unless the leader is willing to look at what skills and time the volunteer brings and how these can be fitted into the program. In volunteer programs, jobs must be tailored to fit the volunteer. Volunteers do learn and develop. In the beginning, though, it is more important to have a volunteer who can do some or most of the job than to continue searching for the perfect person. Do the best you can with what you've got! Refinements will follow.

**Get the most out of your volunteers and their time by effectively using their time.** Volunteers expect their leaders to be as committed to the program as they are. A sign of this commitment from the volunteer's perspective is how organized the leader is. Since volunteers are giving their time, they don't want their time wasted when they come to volunteer. They expect the activity to be organized in advance and materials and equipment to be ready to go when they arrive. (Obviously there are exceptions to this if the volunteer's specific task is to set up the equipment.) The old saying "prior planning prevents poor performance" is particularly important in dealing with volunteers. There is perhaps no better example of poor organization being a time waster than poorly executed meetings.

### *Example*

Ted is the Volunteer Coordinator for the County Youth Soccer Program. He has scheduled a meeting to plan the upcoming soccer season with prospective volunteer coaches. Most of the coaches arrive at or before 7:00

p.m., the scheduled start of the meeting. Ted arrives out of breath and apologizing at 7:10 p.m. He introduces himself, welcomes the coaches, and asks them to introduce themselves. He then goes into a long discussion of the problems that occurred during last year's soccer season, which he hopes to prevent. He finally begins to outline the schedule for the season and which teams will be practicing when and where. Two of the coaches begin talking about problems with playing fields that have drainage problems when it rains. These coaches press Ted to stop using these fields. Ted explains they must use the fields or the number of teams will have to be reduced. Another new coach begins asking questions about officials and their qualifications as he had difficulty with poorly trained officials in another league. By this time there were several side conversations going on and Ted had difficulty bringing the meeting back to the schedule. Once the schedule information was finished, he began sharing ideas about the end of season tournament. The meeting finally ended at 9:45 p.m.

From the coaches' perspective, this meeting was poorly organized, not well led, and was too long. If you are responsible for conducting a meeting, have an agenda in advance, start on time, make sure you have the pertinent information in advance, stick to the agenda, and keep the rest of the attendees on the agenda. End the meeting promptly when the business has been covered. Don't waste your volunteers' time.

**Advance planning and organization prior to the arrival of volunteers are essential.** Volunteers will not continue to support leaders who are disorganized. And leaders who are disorganized seldom enjoy their jobs. Having the activity or work ready to go when the volunteers arrive, lets volunteers know their time is valued by the organization and the volunteer leader. Anticipate problems and give yourself time in advance to solve them. As a leader, you are valuable to the volunteer program and you, too, should be able to enjoy the success of the program and its activities.

Volunteers are part of a team. Most volunteer programs are composed of a number of teams frequently doing different tasks. Leaders must be able to assess the skills and personality styles of individual volunteers and then assign individuals to teams where they will feel comfortable and be able to make their maximum contribution. When putting together teams, obvious personality clashes or differences in style should be avoided, even if it means moving a volunteer to a different team after a few sessions. This is a skill developed over time, but good volunteer leaders understand the importance of building effective teams.

**Effective leaders also understand the necessity of solving problems.** Some problems can be solved fairly easily by getting the facts and taking corrective action. Others, particularly those involving people, can be much more difficult. Too often leaders of volunteer programs fear confronting a problem or an issue to the detriment of the whole program. Avoiding problems seldom makes them go away and, if left unresolved, serious problems will threaten the continued existence of a volunteer program. Volunteer leaders must have the courage to acknowledge that a problem exists, investigate the facts, develop possible courses of action and discuss these with management or the board of directors. When faced with a thorny problem or difficult volunteer, the worst thing you can do is to ignore it. As time passes, the problem will only get worse. If you as the supervisor are aware of it, you can be sure the problem is affecting your other volunteers. Assess the problem, look at both sides of the problem (yours and the volunteer's), make a plan, and then take action. Don't avoid confronting problems.

**Having a thick skin, which is not to be confused with being insensitive, is useful when leading volunteers.** Sometimes volunteers say things to volunteer supervisors in the heat of anger or frustration that they would never think of saying to a boss in the business world. This does not mean volunteers are naturally rude. It does mean that volunteers do not feel as constrained by the structure of a volunteer program as they do in a business setting. As difficult as this may seem, the volunteer leader cannot take outbursts personally. In nearly every case, the volunteer is not really angry at the volunteer leader or the program, although it may certainly seem that way. There is usually something else going on in the person's life that is angering or frustrating them and you and your program just happen to be a convenient target on which to vent their wrath. The problem may be a recent or impending divorce, teenage children, a death in the family, or the threat of downsizing to their paid job. The possibilities are many. If the outburst seems inappropriate to the situation, it probably was not caused by your program or anything you did. Don't take it personally and, most importantly, don't allow yourself to be drawn into an argument.

**Successful leaders look for the best in people, both volunteers and paid staff, in order to continually improve their programs.** They are always recruiting new volunteers and looking for ways to fit volunteers into jobs where they can excel. They are positive leaders. Leaders who feel threatened by the success of their volunteers or who view themselves as better than their volunteers or the people their program serves are doomed to failure. When leaders of volunteers begin referring to volunteers or clients as those idiots or how can he be so stupid, it is time to give that leader another job. In fact, volunteers and clients are not stupid. They pick up on these messages even if the words are not spoken directly to them. While this condescending attitude might work, at least in the short term, with paid employees, it absolutely will not work with volunteers. If your organization is losing volunteers or having difficulty recruiting them, look at leadership style and the respect that your volunteer leader has for the volunteers she leads and the people you serve.

**Leader attitude sets the tone in volunteer programs.** Attitude is contagious. People like to be part of positive, winning teams. They decide whether the volunteer team is a winner largely based on the leader's attitude. Successful leaders, like good coaches, talk up their volunteer team. Complaining about not having enough volunteers or volunteers who fail to show up to work, does nothing positive for the volunteers who are there. In fact it makes them ask the old question, "What does he think I am? Chopped meat?" Complaining doesn't solve problems, but it certainly can create them if the leader's negative attitude rubs off on existing and new volunteers. Volunteer leaders who set a positive tone for their program and look for the best in their volunteers find their volunteers work harder and enjoy their involvement more because they feel they are members of a winning team. If the boss believes in them, how can they lose!

Leading volunteers is much like a card game in which the volunteers hold all the winning cards. In order for the volunteer program to win, the leader must convince the volunteers to play their cards. Volunteers can chose to play their cards or to fold and leave the game. If they fold, they don't lose. The volunteer program loses. You can win big with volunteers, but to do that you must understand the game.

# 9

# KEEPING VOLUNTEERS

**Just because volunteers have signed up and begun working doesn't mean they will continue to volunteer.** In the same way that recruiting is a continuous process, keeping volunteers and developing their skills must be continuous if a volunteer program is to remain viable. Like it or not, good volunteers shop around to find the program that fits them the best. Consequently, they may sign up for several programs before they settle on the one they will stay with. From the volunteer program's point of view, the easy entry level job gives the program's leaders a chance to observe and evaluate a volunteer's potential. It should come as no surprise then that the volunteer is doing the same thing, evaluating the program and its leadership.

**New volunteers must feel from the beginning that they are needed and that their time and skills are valuable.** If, for example, they aren't given anything to do the first time they come to volunteer, they aren't likely to return. They also expect to be treated as individuals with a future in the organization, not just as pawns. Sometimes what can appear to be an efficient way to start all you new volunteers can backfire.

### Example

Darius is fluent in French and Spanish and experienced with international youth exchange programs. A high school guidance counselor, Darius volunteered to work at an international sporting event scheduled to take place for two weeks during the summer. The organizers told him he would be working in the welcome center for international VIPs and he was excited at the prospect. The first meeting of volunteers was held in a convention hall and included over 800 volunteers who had volunteered for a multitude of jobs. Darius found the first meeting highly disorganized. After getting in several lines, he was told to return to be fitted for uniforms. Again hundreds of people were scheduled at the same time, with no improvement in organization. Darius began to ask himself, "Do I want to do this badly enough to stand in this long line again?" He called his point of contact with the organizers, who then scheduled a smaller meeting with Darius and several other volunteers with similar backgrounds, who would be working in the Welcome Center. At that time, Darius was told the total number of days he would be required to work, effectively his whole four week summer vacation. Based on his experience to date with the organization, Darius decided not to volunteer at all and left with a bad overall impression of the organization.

### The process of keeping volunteers starts with their first impressions as new volunteers.

Volunteers are regularly evaluating the volunteer program to determine whether it is worthwhile to continue giving their time. They must be able to see a direct connection between their contributions and making a difference for the cause or the clients the program serves.

Volunteers give their time individually, even though they may work in groups, and they expect to be treated as valuable individuals. Take time to learn their names. Dale Carnegie said it best: "Remember that a man's name is to him the sweetest and most important sound in the English language." If you have difficulty remembering names, use name tags. It's ok to cheat here. Even the military uses name tags so that people become known by their names. Find out what the volunteer likes to be called and use that name, more than just to call the roll. It is worth noting that not everyone likes to be called by his first name. Some folks prefer to be called Mister Jones rather than Darrell. Respect the person's choice. While this is very basic, it sends a strong message to the volunteer about his value. Calling him by his name tells him he is an important part of the team.

**When a volunteer begins with an entry level job, you get the chance to see them in action.**
If they appear to be someone with potential as a volunteer, ask them back. As obvious as this may seem, it is often overlooked. Make it a point to ask the volunteer to return for a specific time and date. Just saying, "We hope you will come back." is not enough. Be specific. You want them to know they are needed and you would welcome their return. Let them know what you want them to do, where, and when. If they decline or waffle, give them another date or time which may be more convenient. Some volunteers may still hedge and you may decide this is not a person you wish to pursue. If, however, you think they have a lot to contribute and would enjoy your program, give them a phone call in a few days to thank them for coming and to repeat the invitation to a specific future event. If you don't make it a point to invite people back, many will say they enjoyed volunteering with your program, but will never return.

There may be some volunteers whom you can tell from their first work in an entry level job, will have a limited future with your program, either because of their style or their expectations. If it does not appear they will be able to contribute or will enjoy working with your program, thank them for their work and just don't ask them to come back. Make it a habit to thank volunteers for their contributions regularly. Find something good about what they are doing and praise them for it. For example, "Wanda, your patience with the children is really making a difference. I'm so glad you decided to volunteer with us." Note, this is different from the rather automatic and less sincere, "Thanks for volunteering today." as a person departs. While a pleasant sentiment, such impersonal comments are the equivalent of the convenience store clerk saying, "Have a nice day." Volunteers who stay need to know they are valuable to the program as individuals, not just as a generic volunteer. Take time to call volunteers or drop them a short hand written note, postcard, or E-mail after they have volunteered to say thanks. These do not have to be long. They do need to be sincere and address what the volunteer did. These can come from volunteer supervisors, not just the Volunteer Coordinator. If you want good volunteers to continue giving you their time, give them a little of your time in saying thank you.

**While volunteers should start in entry level jobs, don't leave them in these jobs, unless that is their preference.** Get to know each volunteer as an individual with unique strengths and abilities. Start talking to them about other jobs you think they might enjoy doing (and which, coincidentally, you also need done). To get the most benefit from volunteers, you must match them to jobs they enjoy and are comfortable doing. This may mean offering them additional training, more responsibility, different hours, or a different job site. Actively seek the best fit for the volunteer within your organization. Just as you don't want to leave volunteers in entry level jobs indefinitely, you must regularly look for new ways to stimulate interest and energy in dedicated volunteers.

## Example

Tina started out volunteering as an escort for prospective adoptive families at Cocker Spaniel Rescue adoption days. She had had a cocker as a child. Now she was living in an apartment and her cocker was still with her parents in New Jersey. She missed her dog and saw helping rescue as a way to stay in contact with dogs. Tina was enthusiastic and a quick learner. Soon she was asked to do home checks for families asking to adopt dogs.

Her interpersonal skills and conscientious follow up were exceptional. The program coordinator asked her if she would be interested in helping answer the voice mail calls, normally five to ten per day. She jumped at the chance. As it turned out, she was unhappy in her paid job and saw her work with rescue as a way to achieve more personal satisfaction. She did a superb job with the voice mail. She then offered to serve as a foster family for an incoming senior dog, one of the most difficult volunteer jobs to fill. Recognizing Tina's skills and potential not only kept her involved with the program, it also gave the program an increasingly valuable volunteer.

To keep volunteers active, you must involve them in the program beyond just doing a job. Volunteers are more than robotic laborers. They have insight, ideas and experience which they will contribute if they believe they are an important part of the program. Capitalize on their skills by making them integral parts of your program and giving them jobs that challenge and reward them.

**Recognize the volunteer's underlying motivation for volunteering and make sure you are meeting their need.** Depending on your organization, a varying percentage will be motivated by pure altruism, an unselfish desire to help others or to promote a cause. These individuals must see a direct link between what they are doing as a volunteer and the results with people or the cause your program serves. Sometimes this link is easy to demonstrate and reinforce as in the case of Big Brothers or Big Sisters. The volunteer has direct contact with the young person. In other cases the volunteer may be putting together materials for other volunteers to use in working with clients. In both cases it is the job of the program coordinator to ensure that each volunteer sees the results of his or her efforts. This can be done by personal comments, for example, the parent or teacher telling the volunteer how much the child's behavior and grades have improved. Selected comments from parents, teachers, or other members of the community about the success of children in the program written in newsletters, for example, can show all volunteers the impact of their efforts.

**Look at the reason or reasons the volunteer signed up to volunteer in the beginning and be certain you are meeting their expectations.** If they signed up because they wanted to meet people, are they actually getting to do that or are they restricted in their contacts to just a few other volunteers? If they volunteered because there was something in it for them, are they getting what they wanted? If they are volunteering because the boss said do it, does their boss know from you how well they are doing? Although you would hope to go beyond the volunteer's initial motivation by involving the volunteer in your program, you must first meet their initial goals.

For some volunteers, once their goals have been met they tend to stop volunteering. This is particularly true with volunteers motivated because there's something in it for them. For example, when their child has outgrown scouting, they are unlikely to continue as a troop leader. Similarly, if the volunteer's ultimate goal in volunteering was to be seen and to make connections that would facilitate their being invited to join a particular club, once they have been invited to join the club they probably will not continue to volunteer with your program. Appreciate these volunteers while you have them. Even your best efforts are unlikely to keep them as long term volunteers.

**The lives and schedules of all volunteers change.** Good volunteers often leave programs because they can no longer fit their volunteer work into their schedule. Keeping these good volunteers requires anticipation of these changes, which is easier when you know your volunteers as individuals. Subtle signs may be a regular volunteer who gradually starts missing her scheduled volunteer day, even though she may call you in advance to tell you she cannot come. It may show in volunteers who leave early or just as soon as their shift is over without stopping to exchange pleasantries with others before leaving.

Whatever the warning signs, recognizing them is critical. Talk to the volunteer about how much you value her dedicated work and your concern that something else may be making it difficult for her to volunteer. It's not important to identify what is taking her time. After all, you are not criticizing her, or at least you shouldn't be. Offer the volunteer a way to change how she volunteers. This almost always means a different job or different hours. It may mean giving two volunteers the chance to share one volunteer job with each working every other week rather than once a week. Let the volunteer know her experience and contributions are valuable and that you are willing to be flexible in order to keep her as a volunteer. How hard you wish to work this depends on how important the particular volunteer is to your program.

**Giving volunteers a chance to take a break from volunteering is risky, but can be used effectively provided the volunteer is kept involved in the program, if only from the point of communication.** Keep them informed of what is going on, progress of the program, and who is involved. Regularly remind them of their value to the program and how much you would like to see them return. This latter point is the one most often overlooked. Periodically offer volunteers taking a break a chance to re-enter the volunteer force by inviting them to participate in activities with a short time commitment.

### *Example*

Carlos had been very active in the community children's garden program. After five years he felt burned out and asked for a break. He was kept informed of the program's activities and invited to planning sessions. After five months he was invited back to be a judge at the children's Spring Garden Show. Carlos really enjoyed being called back as an expert. After the show, he spent time talking with the children whose gardens had been runners up and suggesting ways they might improve their plots for the Fall Garden Show. The program coordinator asked Carlos if he would consider volunteering just the month prior to the garden shows to help children interested in competing prepare their plots. This was a change in commitment for Carlos, who had previously been a group leader committed to working every Saturday with a group of ten children. As a result, Carlos returned to volunteering but in a different role.

Keeping good volunteers is really nothing more than valuing their contributions, letting them know you appreciate what they do, incorporating them into your program where they can make their best contribution and still enjoy it, and meeting their needs. Good volunteers are priceless. Keep them by treating them as valuable members of the team.

# 10

# RECOGNITION AND REWARDS

Volunteers thrive on appreciation. Appreciation is, after all, the only pay they get. Thanking them once a year at the annual volunteer recognition luncheon is not enough. Volunteers who feel their contributions and time are not appreciated or are being taken for granted will stop volunteering. Few of them will ever tell you why.

**To be most effective, appreciation must be personal.** The best forms are in person thank you's, phone calls, and personal handwritten notes. These do not have to be long, however, they should be prompt and personal. Call the person by name and thank them specifically for what they are doing or have done. Take time to thank your new volunteers in particular — it keeps them coming back. A thank you phone call might go something like this.

### Example

"Mike, I really appreciated your help with the camporee last weekend. Getting those boys who wanted to race around on their own to participate in the evening campfire was a big help. We need more volunteers like you. I look forward to working with you again. I'll give you a call next month to let you know when the meeting will be. Hope you will be able to join us."

The exact words are less important than three points:

**1)** thank you,

**2)** you made a difference on our team, and

**3)** an invitation to return.

These messages are of course best when delivered directly to the volunteer, but they can also be effective left on the answering machine or with a responsible family member. Telling the wife how great her husband is gets the message across and also adds a friend to your network. As for the answering machine, positive messages that don't require a return call are a pleasant surprise.

A similarly worded hand written thank you note or post card is also effective. Three or four sentences are usually sufficient. Mass produced, individually addressed notes printed on a word processor may be tempting. After all, they are fast and professional looking. Unfortunately, the average volunteer, who has received plenty of personalized junk mail, will recognize these for what they are — cheap and mass produced. The sincerity and personal touch of a hand written note makes a difference, even if it is signed by the volunteer supervisor rather than the head of the organization. The following example is of a mass produced thank you letter.

### Example:

Dear Volunteer Safe Boating Instructor:

Thanks for your help in making it possible for us to host the 16th annual Boating Safety Saturday.

The event was a great success! In the metropolitan area a grand total of 578 individuals were certified in Boating Safety! Nearly 75 volunteers worked together that day to ensure the success of the event. It couldn't have happened without a great deal of dedicated support from instructors like you, who provided much needed success in our boating community.

On behalf of the Tarpon Power Fleet, I thank you. Please call if this office can be of any assistance to you.

Sincerely,

(signed) Volunteer Coordinator

Compare this with the next example of a handwritten note.

### Example: Personal note

Sam,

Thank you so much for the great work you did with the Harrison County Institute of Gardening Knowledge. I have had so much positive feed back from your last class!

I am honored to be associated with such fine people as you and the Harrison County Master Gardeners.

Sincerely,

(signed) Volunteer Coordinator

**Not all notes and calls need to be made by the Volunteer Coordinator.** They can be decentralized to others. They must, however, be done by someone who knows the volunteer and has personal knowledge of what the volunteer has done. How often appreciation is expressed varies. It is most important in the beginning and then can be less frequent as volunteers become established in the program, perhaps once a month. Communicating sincere thank you's to volunteers is a case where more is better. Don't assume you have thanked someone enough. Volunteers who have gotten enough thank you's will tell you. Even experienced volunteers who have been with you for months or years need to be thanked regularly. Thanking volunteers is not hard to do. In fact it can make the person saying thank you feel even better about the program and the volunteers. Unfortunately, in the scramble to get things done, saying thank you is easy to forget.

Publicity in the form of newspaper or television coverage, newsletters, and Internet web pages are another way to recognize and thank volunteers. Local newspapers are often glad to publish information about your program and your volunteers, especially if you make it easy for them by providing photographs and a short write-up. Prompt submission to newspapers is vital. If it has been several weeks since the event occurred, your information is no longer news. People like to see their pictures and names in the paper, your newsletter, or on the Internet. Their friends also see it and tell them.

**As valuable as publicity is, it only recognizes those volunteers who are pictured or named.** There is no transference to the rest of the volunteers. A newsletter entry that says, "We would like to thank all our volunteers who helped with the food drive," doesn't do much. It might make the writer or newsletter editor feel good, but it is not personal. It does nothing to thank specific volunteers. Obviously listing every volunteer's name is one way of resolving the problem. The risk here is of leaving out someone's name or including the name of someone who didn't show up. This is why the personal phone call or written note is so important.

**Appreciation must be personal.** Many organizations give out T-shirts, tote bags, or baseball caps, for example, to recognize their volunteers and as tokens of appreciation. Lots of people enjoy and collect these items and they do attract new volunteers. These are especially useful with one day or short term volunteer events. Give aways have their place. They are good publicity for your organization. But to use them as your only expression of thanks to long term volunteers fails to demonstrate the value your organization should be placing on the contributions of volunteers as individuals. There are ways to make these items both publicity and personal recognition.

### Example

Goodwill Industries holds a large annual used book sale. Many volunteers are used both to sort donated books and to work at the sale itself. Every volunteer who works 18 hours or more during the year receives a personal thank you and a useable token of appreciation. The first year they receive a cloth shop apron with their name embroidered on it. For every subsequent year they receive a unique patch to sew onto their apron. Not only do the volunteers wear these aprons with pride while working, the aprons also serve to identify volunteer staff members to customers at the book sale. Coincidentally, the aprons serve as name tags, too.

It takes more effort to personalize the T-shirts, tote bags, and baseball caps with associated costs in terms of money and time. For a one time volunteer event, mass produced items make sense. They are most effective when they are an adjunct to rather than a substitute for a personal word of thanks, phone call, or note.

Tokens of appreciation in conjunction with a personal note of thanks are often used to good effect at the annual volunteer luncheon or dinner. In some cases the gifts are donated and in others they are purchased. In every case, though, the token of appreciation should fit the volunteer's contribution.

### Example

Jasmine is an exceptional volunteer who has worked 1,100 hours over the past year at the Chamber of Commerce Visitors' Center. Her contributions have been particularly noteworthy because of her language abilities and the large number of international businesses visiting the city during the year. At the annual volunteer recognition reception, she was thanked and presented a large bottle of bubble bath as a token of appreciation.

In view of the number of hours this volunteer had given, this particular token of appreciation appeared at best to be an after thought. Make the token of appreciation, if you chose to use one, fit the individual's volunteer contributions. In the end, though, intangible rewards are more valuable to the volunteer than any material gift.

**Periodic events to honor volunteers are a valuable part of rewards and recognition.** Like T-shirts, though, they should be personalized rather than mass gatherings with a general speech by the organization's president thanking all the volunteers for their terrific work this past year. It's not necessary to read off every volunteer's name. Rather, recognize individually those volunteers whose contributions have been exceptional. You may give them a plaque or other token of appreciation or you may not. The remaining volunteers can be recognized for their contributions in groups.

### Example

"We would now like to recognize the wonderful volunteers who keep the nursery during church services. Many of us never get to see you on Sundays to say thanks in person. Would you please stand so that we may all see who you are? (Applause)

Volunteer Sunday School teachers are so important to
our program. We would like to offer a special thanks to
those of you who spend time during the week preparing
the lessons and teaching classes to our young people.
Would all the Youth Division Sunday School teachers
please stand so that we may recognize you? (Applause)

The positive impact of recognition events can be further
enhanced by the president, Volunteer Coordinator, and
volunteer supervisors making a special effort to circulate
through the crowd at the event and thank volunteers individually. When the volunteers are with their family or
friends, the value of these public thank you's multiplies.
Unfortunately, the tendency after the luncheon concludes is
for the leaders to huddle together to discuss problems or
future programs. Resist the temptation! The pay off for a
few words of personal thanks here will be enormous in
volunteer retention and in volunteers encouraging their
friends to join your program.

**In addition to being thanked by the program's
leaders, volunteers also receive great satisfaction through seeing the results of their work.**
Hospital volunteers see patients brighten when they come
in to bring the mail or the book cart. USO volunteers see
first hand the appreciation of service members and their
families when they are helped in USO airport lounges. The
recipients of their volunteer work regularly thank them.
There is no substitute for this hands on contact and the
personal exchanges with people affected by the volunteer
program. If you have volunteers who normally work behind
the scenes, occasionally ask them to participate in the
hands on contact portion of your program, or at least let
them see the volunteer work taking place. When clients
send you thank you letters, circulate the letters around so

that everyone gets to read them. Put them on the bulletin board or in the newsletter. Every volunteer is important to the team and deserves to share in this recognition.

### Example

Volunteers with Habitat for Humanity see the results of their work as they watch the house they are building take shape. The individual or family for whom the house is being built works on the construction, too, so the volunteers get to know the people who will directly benefit from their work. When the house is completed, all the volunteers who worked on the house are invited back for its dedication.

**Another way to reward volunteers is to expand their responsibility or promote them.** This might sound contradictory - giving people more work as a reward. The fact is people appreciate having their abilities acknowledged and their contributions expanded. Obviously a promotion or increase in responsibility should fit the individual volunteer. When you know your volunteers well, you also know who will respond to this kind of reward.

### Example

Chris has been an excellent volunteer firefighter for over two years. He is reliable, hard working, and has good interpersonal skills. In recognition of his abilities and potential, Chris is asked to join the training team for new volunteers.

Just as additional responsibility can be a reward, so can additional training. Some people volunteer specifically because of the training offered to volunteers. Others see additional training and opportunities to learn as a bonus for doing a good job as a volunteer. Clearly, offering someone training that is required or of little interest to them is not a reward. Training that expands their knowledge in a field they enjoy and that is relevant to their volunteer job can be a definite bonus.

### Example

The Museum of Art uses volunteers to conduct museum tours. Once volunteers have passed their introductory and probation period, they are given the opportunity to conduct tours one morning a week and to attend additional training on another morning each week. This additional training is on new exhibits coming to the museum, as well as more in depth information on a variety of artists. Idalia, who has been volunteering with the museum for over ten years, says that while she enjoys taking school groups on tours, her specialty, she really appreciates the weekly training and getting to view the various exhibits for free. She sees it as an opportunity to continually expand her knowledge and appreciation of fine art.

**Reward your good volunteers by showing them off when you have distinguished visitors or an invitation to talk to a group about your program.** Parents understand the value of showing off their children when they do well. The same principle applies to volunteers. With successful volunteer programs, the Volunteer Coordinator often gets tired of having to give the dog and pony show for visitors. This is a great opportunity to shine the spotlight on a good volunteer. Let him tell about the program. Because of their personal commitment and enthusiasm, volunteers can do these talks well. They also feel you have recognized their contributions and ability by asking them to give the talk.

Including good volunteers in planning your program is another way to reward them. They see your program differently than you do and they have a definite stake in its success. Many times volunteers will see a possible course of action or solution to the problem you may have overlooked. When they are included in planning and proposed changes to the program, volunteers know leadership appreciates their contributions and values their ideas. Volunteers who have had a part in developing the plan are much more likely to support it than those who are just told this is the way we are going to do it.

**Finally there is appreciation for the work of volunteers who leave your program.** Of course, most people think of the classic farewell luncheon for Miss Bessie who has been a Red Cross volunteer for 52 years and is moving away to live in a retirement community. These events are familiar and most organizations do them well. But what about the people who have been good volunteers with your program for a year or more and then suddenly stop coming? It is tempting to just cross them off and forget them. As a minimum, if someone has been a regular volunteer and then just stops coming, the volunteer supervisor should call them to see if they are sick or some other problem has occurred. These volunteers have been valuable to your program. Let them know that by expressing your concern that they are no longer volunteering.

**Resist the temptation to express your frustration, even if you feel they have left you in the proverbial lurch.** Dedicated people usually have a good reason when they stop volunteering. They may be sick, have had a death in the family, been put on another shift, lost their job, etc. There is also the possibility they are not happy with your program. If that is the case, give them a chance to explain what they are unhappy with. Take time to listen to them without arguing. Perhaps it is a misunderstanding, boredom with their volunteer job, scheduling, or something else you can resolve. In any event, you and the volunteer have a lot invested in experience and time. Give her a chance to explain her position. If the situation is such that the volunteer will not be returning, take time to sincerely thank her for all the volunteer work she has done with your program. This can be done verbally or in a short note.

### *Example*

Leann had been a faithful volunteer for over a year at the humane society. She had even recruited her mother to volunteer. Suddenly they both stopped coming on their scheduled day. Their supervisor called them to find out if anything was wrong, but only got their answering machine and never had his calls returned. He reported this to the Director of the Humane Society. The director wrote a personal note to Leann and her mother. "We miss your hard work and enthusiasm at the shelter. Although I do not know what has happened in your lives, I do hope that whatever it is it will be resolved soon. You have both done a terrific job with the Humane Society and I want to thank you on behalf of everyone in the organization. If your situation changes so that you can return, we would be delighted to have you rejoin us."

**Letting volunteers know you appreciate their work even when they leave your program has far reaching impact.** First, the person may be feeling somewhat guilty that they have left. You help them save face by saying thank you. Second, if they have been good volunteers, you would like then to return as volunteers even if they have to take a break in volunteering. Third, if you are a nonprofit program, these former volunteers may continue to donate money to your program. Finally, you want them to speak well of your program to others. A few minutes spent saying thanks can get you credible word of mouth advertising and support you cannot buy at any price. Volunteers need to know you care about them and you appreciate their contributions.

# 11

# DEALING WITH PROBLEM VOLUNTEERS

Properly placed, coached, and reinforced
relatively few volunteers become problems. Volunteers who
are unhappy with the organization or structure can and do
leave of their own volition. As often as not, this is the way
most problem volunteers are dealt with. Intentionally
leaving a problem volunteer out of the information and
appreciation system can be an effective way to encourage
them to stop volunteering. However, this should only be
done when all the facts are known and a decision has been
made that the program would be better off without this
volunteer. The more difficult problems are with dedicated
volunteers, who participate regularly and may be quite
vocal. You may think, "You cannot fire a volunteer.", but
there are ways to deal with them so that problem volunteers
do not destroy your program or your sanity.

### Determine exactly what the problem is.
Sometimes people are labeled as problem volunteers when
they are not really the problem. Often the report of a
problem volunteer is exaggerated or based on an isolated
incident. When you receive a report of this type or a series
of complaints, investigate to get all the facts before taking
action. The volunteer may be sick, have had a bad day at
work or have had family problems. Perhaps the volunteer is
not aware that what she is doing runs counter to the organization's policies or that she is irritating people. Taking

---

action prematurely risks losing a good volunteer. Ask questions and avoid joining in the general grousing about the volunteer's behavior. Listen, listen, listen before you act. Occasionally the real problem may be the individual who is complaining, but more often it is that the volunteer is unaware of what she is doing or should be doing.

Getting the facts will generally require a talk with the volunteer in private. After telling the volunteer he is important to the success of the program, you must directly address what you perceive as the problem. Listen to the volunteer's side and any solutions he may propose. He may solve the problem for you at this point. If not, be prepared to suggest ways to resolve the problem or change the behavior. Be as flexible as you can to new ideas or ways of doing the job. Sometimes the volunteer will decide to quit at this point. More frequently they, too, will have been uncomfortable with the situation and will welcome a chance to clear the air and resolve the problem. A better and more dedicated volunteer can be the ultimate outcome.

**Problem volunteers can be the result of being placed in jobs poorly suited to their skills or personality.** For example, some people thrive on physical work while others are more comfortable working with administration. Occasionally problem volunteers are actually bored with their job or looking for more responsibility and challenge. They may be chaffing under a supervisor whose style does not mesh with theirs. The root of the problem is not always obvious from the behavior or the reports you receive. Talking with and listening to volunteers will reveal these underlying causes.

**Volunteers who are late or don't come at all can be an irritant, especially to volunteer**

**supervisors.** Has the supervisor clearly explained the schedule to the volunteer? Did the volunteer get a chance to say, "I can't come then or I will be late," or was it just assumed she would be there? Some people need to be reminded of when they are expected, while others are habitually late. Unless your volunteers come the same day each week, it can be useful to call volunteers a few days before the event at which they are scheduled to work to invite them and to remind them of the day and time. Be sure the volunteer knows that he is valuable to the program and is making a difference. If the volunteer is working with clients, use the clients as a reason to come reliably and on time. For example, "Ken, when the children get here at three o'clock, they are looking for you to begin. It means a lot to them to see you here and ready to go. They are disappointed in you when you aren't here." In this way, telling him he is needed at a set time has relevance. Telling him that you need him there only has relevance to the volunteer if you are important to him.

**For those volunteers who are habitually late, look first at the situation.** Are you and your program organized so the volunteer can start right to work when she arrives or does it take you 15 or 20 minutes to get things set up after the agreed upon start time? Does the volunteer have a meaningful job which she enjoys doing? If the volunteer feels you are wasting her time at the beginning of each work session or not using her talents appropriately, it is only natural for her to drag her feet and arrive late. Would the volunteer be more comfortable with a different work schedule? After you have ruled out these reasons, if the volunteer is still habitually late then it makes sense to assign them a job where punctuality is not an issue, that is, the work can be done at any time. With some people, no matter how much you stress being on time, they just aren't prompt. To keep this type of volunteer, you and your program must be flexible.

**Volunteers who fail to follow through on commitments are aggravating.** Following up to see if they are all right and to find out why they missed their commitment is essential before crossing them off your list and swearing you will never give them a responsible job again. Sometimes people do have sickness or car trouble, etc. When people know you care and are going to check, they tend to be more reliable. If there is a pattern of not following through with commitments and there is no underlying reason, give the volunteer other jobs to do where they are not critical to the success of the project. Do not make these volunteers supervisors.

Volunteers who come unprepared are a common distraction in programs, particularly if the volunteer is in a leadership position. Again, get the facts. Does the person know what is expected and how it relates to the success of the program as a whole? If not, it is the volunteer supervisor's responsibility to explain this and to make preparation relevant.

### *Example*

Stu is a Little League baseball equipment manager. Practices are supposed to start at four o'clock and Stu usually rolls up right at four. Unfortunately more often than not he arrives without bats, bases, and practice balls. He then has to send someone to his house, (usually Robert, one of the assistant coaches) to get the missing equipment. As a result, practices start and end late and all the teams waste nearly 30 minutes waiting for the equipment. Robert and several of the coaches have complained to John, the Little League Coordinator. John drops in on the next practice and sees the missing equipment scenario himself. Overall Stu is an experienced volunteer, who has good rapport with the coaches and the players. John hates to lose Stu as he has no one else willing to take on the job. Rather than unloading on Stu for being irresponsible, he talks to him in private after the practice is over. He begins with the potential of the program and the children and Stu's value to the league. He then addresses the pattern of missing equipment at practice and explains to Stu that these wasted 30 minutes could be the difference between keeping coaches and parents happy and involved. It could also prevent dissension and problems experienced by many leagues. John relates the problem to the people and the program, which he knows are important to Stu.

**Problems with volunteers and preparedness can also be more individual,** such as the hospital volunteer who regularly forgets her name tag or uniform smock. In these situations you have to decide which is more important, having the volunteer there and working or the details of appearance. In most programs what the volunteer does is more important than appearance. If there are cogent reasons, such as security, that require the name tag or smock, explain that to the volunteer. If the problem persists and the volunteer is valuable to your program (and most volunteers who come regularly are valuable), look for other ways to solve the problem such as temporary name tags or additional smocks to loan to those who forget theirs. Volunteers have different personality styles. While most volunteers are team players, some have personality styles that challenge the healthy team concept. For example, some volunteers in youth sports have as a primary goal winning at all costs with no regard for development of the children's skills or sportsmanship. Some volunteers in leadership positions are on personal ego trips. Volunteers who say the first thing that pops into their mind without considering its impact on others can be especially disruptive, as can volunteers with volatile tempers. Perhaps the most common personality style that causes problems in volunteer programs is the volunteer who must control every detail of the work being done. Often these are volunteers who have been with the program for a long time and are hard workers.

### Example

Nancy was in charge of consignments for the thrift shop. She was a dedicated worker, who had been a thrift shop volunteer for over five years. Nancy had seen a lot of volunteers come and go and in her mind she knew how the work should be done. She dismissed new ideas with "We did that once and it didn't work.", whether the idea had ever been tried before or not. She was appointed to her present position because of her experience and because she was a tireless worker. Unfortunately, few of the volunteers in her section shared her style or worked exactly like Nancy did. She regularly upbraided volunteers in front of customers for not listing the condition of items being consigned, a measure she had initiated. Several of the volunteers had difficulty with this point because items which appeared to them to be in poor condition were, according to the customers consigning them, in like new condition. Nancy often got so frustrated with her volunteers that she would push them aside and take over the work herself. The thrift shop manager was reluctant to confront Nancy as Nancy had volunteered for so many years and because, frankly, she was a little afraid of Nancy's wrath being turned on her. As the months dragged by, fewer and fewer volunteers continued to work for Nancy. They left with lame excuses that they just didn't have time or their husbands were about to be transferred. Nancy complained more and more to the thrift shop manager that she had to do all the work herself. She just wasn't getting any decent volunteers.

Particularly in small all volunteer programs, a disruptive volunteer like Nancy can cripple an otherwise effective volunteer program. Ultimately, failure to recognize and address the problem volunteer can destroy a program by driving away good volunteers. After all, who wants to work in an environment like this if they don't have to? Before attacking this type of problem, you must assess the risk. Could addressing the problem cause the problem volunteer or other volunteers, possibly her close friends, to leave? Would the organization be better or worse off in the long run without her? Can the organization survive without her? Ultimately the decision has to be made by management, preferably with the knowledge and support of the board of directors.

Once the decision has been made that, if worse comes to worse and the volunteer quits as a result of being confronted, the organization will survive, the way is clear if not easy. The Volunteer Coordinator or board of directors must talk directly to the problem volunteer in private, outline the behavior that is unacceptable and explain why. Use specific examples. Listen to the volunteer's explanation and any proposed corrective action he may make. No matter how angry or abusive the volunteer may become at this stage, do not get drawn into an argument. Just listen. If cogent new facts have been introduced, consider modifying your planned course of action. If not, wait until the volunteer runs out of steam and stops talking. This may take a while, but not so long if you don't respond. Conclude the session by thanking him for his work in the past and telling him in simple straight forward language that the board of directors has decided his behavior is not acceptable and that he is no longer needed as a volunteer. Expect a rebuttal from the volunteer, but remain steady in your position.

### *Example*

Phil was a hard working volunteer with a debt counseling program. In addition to being dedicated to the clients of the program, he was very opinionated about how things should be run. He had voiced his opinions to the board of directors and to anyone else who would listen. A few but not all of his ideas had been adopted. Phil was unwilling to conform to the decisions of the board. He began telling, not only other volunteers, but clients as well, that individuals on the board didn't know what they were doing and didn't really care about the clients' welfare. His attacks became very rude and personal in phone calls with members of the board. Overall morale among the volunteers was threatened as rumors abounded.

After several heated replies from Phil in response to fairly routine questions, the board invited him to a board meeting. He was given an opportunity to voice his opinions without opposition. The board had agreed in advance that no one would contest Phil's statements or argue with him. Phil was then told that the organization did not appear to be meeting his goals. He was also told that the majority of the group had elected the board and the board was not going to change its procedures. It was explained to Phil that his rude comments would not be tolerated. The board president recounted Phil's strengths and suggested the only way for Phil to get the program he was proposing would be to set one up himself using his own ideas. Phil left the meeting fuming and several days later sent in his letter of resignation from the group. He subsequently formed a small debt counseling program of his own. Following this meeting and Phil's subsequent departure, overall morale among the volunteers improved dramatically. Several volunteers quietly told the president they had been considering quitting because of Phil's behavior.

**Allow the former problem volunteer, now essentially fired, to save face and leave before telling others about the decision.** Rumors travel with lightning speed in volunteer programs. It is therefore very important that the Volunteer Coordinator or board of directors tell the other volunteers the problem volunteer will no longer be working with the program. It is not necessary to go into great detail about why. Expect some turmoil as people get used to the idea. Very shortly, though, the program will right itself and move on. When a very serious problem volunteer has come to the attention of management, you can be certain that individual has been a problem to other volunteers as well. Removing a source of irritation will produce rapid healing, provided all the facts were obtained prior to the decision and the actual firing was done courteously and in private.

**While organizations dread the serious problem volunteer, the fact is most volunteers are great performers provided they get the information, coaching, and encouragement they need.** The importance of matching the job to the volunteer's personality and style cannot be over emphasized. An appropriate job match can eliminate many potential problems with volunteers before they even begin. To do this, though, programs must be flexible and leaders have to know their volunteers as individuals. The decision to ask a volunteer to leave the program should be a last resort.

# 12

# WHY GOOD VOLUNTEERS QUIT

Some reasons good volunteers quit are beyond the control of the volunteer program, such as moving to another town or a child who has lost interest in youth soccer where mom was a volunteer coach. Many of the reasons, however, are within the purview of the volunteer program's leadership and can be corrected before a volunteer quits. It's worth reviewing the most common reasons people give for quitting a volunteer program.

➤ **They just don't have enough time.** If you ask the question, this is the most common response you will get. In nearly every case this is a socially acceptable answer which leaves out the rest of the sentence, I just don't have enough time to be doing work I don't enjoy anymore. Look beyond the not enough time reason to find the real reason.

➤ **No one appreciates what they do.** In this category are volunteers who do their work quietly and efficiently day after day. Other than possibly clients, no one in a leadership position in the organization ever says thank you. No one ever asks for their ideas or if they would like to do something different other than the job they are now doing. From their perspective, nobody cares so why should they? These volunteers feel they are being taken for granted and their contributions are not appreciated. These volunteers will rarely tell you this directly.

### ➤ They are tired of having their time wasted.

Volunteers who are giving their time expect that time to be used productively. They get frustrated when they come on time ready to work only to have to wait for the program's leaders to get organized and get the work started. They get discouraged when they must attend meetings that go on for hours and never accomplish anything. These volunteers understand last minute changes, but they don't expect them to be routine. In short, they are giving their time and they expect the program to use their time efficiently. When their time is repeatedly wasted, they decide it's not worth their while to continue volunteering.

### ➤ They don't feel they are making a difference.

Volunteers who cannot see the effect of their work become disenchanted. This is a common problem with repetitive and administrative tasks. Unless the organization can regularly show them how their work is making a difference for the people or the cause the program serves, behind the scenes volunteers can lose interest. Volunteers who have personal contact with clients can also be affected.

### *Example*

Ron volunteered as a literacy tutor in a county adult literacy program. Ron's first experience was teaching a woman, who as it turned out could already read. The woman even brought in books she was reading. Her problem was that she was not comprehending what she read. After spending time explaining that she had to think about what she read and asking her questions about material she had read, Ron felt the woman really did not need literacy tutoring. He talked to his volunteer supervisor about it and was given a different client. The next person he was assigned to tutor was a man in prison. At first Ron was excited at the prospect of making a difference in this man's life. Gradually, though, he realized the man could already read. He didn't need tutoring. In fact, the man had just told people he couldn't read in order to get a break from the prison routine.

## ➤ They feel they are doing the work all alone and not getting any support.

Most common in volunteers who lead activities, particularly youth programs, this problem does not surface over night. These are usually volunteers who care about the program and the people it serves, are dedicated, and hard working. They want the program to succeed. Over time, though, they become disillusioned because they feel they are carrying the load alone.

### Example

Kevin had been a Eagle Scout and had volunteered as a Boy Scout troop leader. He enjoyed the out of doors and was experienced with hiking and camping. The troop was growing and the boys and their parents were enthusiastic about the scouts' projects and the number of badges they were earning. Initially parents had been outspoken in saying they would support the troop, but somehow they were often too busy when work needed to be done. No one from the council talked to Kevin except to say they were pleased with how much he was doing with the troop. Things all came to a head when the troop planned a four day hike on the Appalachian Trail. Kevin said they could do it, but only if he had five other adults to help. Five parents volunteered. On the first day of the hike, all the boys showed up, but only one father arrived to help. He was needed to drive the resupply truck, which he did. This left Kevin on his own in charge of 12 boys on the trail. Rather than disappoint the boys, Kevin conducted the hike as planned. Fortunately no serious problems arose while on the trail. After he returned, Kevin called the council and gave them a four week notice that he would no longer be a troop leader.

By the time this problem reaches the point the volunteer is ready to quit, there may be no salvaging the situation. It is imperative for leaders of volunteers to stay in close communication with their volunteers to prevent this type of frustration and burnout. If Kevin's supervisor had been aware of the problems in advance, he might have been able to help Kevin prevent the no show situation. After all, lack of parental support is not a new problem with youth groups. Just telling the parents and boys in advance that if five parents did not show up to assist with the hike, the hike would not take place would have upped the ante for the parents and put pressure on them to follow through with their commitments. As it was, Kevin did not have the experience to know this should be done. He expected all adults to be as responsible as he was. Neither the organization nor the parents gave him the support he needed. The organization lost an otherwise fine volunteer as a result.

➤ **They don't get any of the credit.** These are generally hard working volunteers who have enjoyed what they do and believe the program makes a difference. Their frustration centers around their supervisor and their supervisor's boss, who are quick to take credit for the volunteers' good ideas and hard work, but keep the real workers in the background. When there is praise to be handed out, the supervisor is always up front to receive it. This leadership style on the supervisor's part can unwittingly cost the program good volunteers. Management needs to be aware of and take corrective action when leaders never acknowledge their subordinates or bring them forward to receive the credit and praise.

> **They are tired of being told exactly how to do everything.** Sometimes there are good reasons for strict inflexible procedures. More often, though, these are a result of habit and inflexible leaders who have to control every detail of the work. Some volunteers will tolerate this, but many will chafe under this kind of control. They want to know the objective of the procedure and the general parameters in which it must be done. After they have done it by the rules for a while, they would like to improve the process if they can. Listen to these volunteers. They can be your future leaders. Some of their ideas may not work, but, if possible, let them try their ideas. If it's not possible to try their ideas, take time to listen to them and then explain why their idea cannot be implemented. If volunteers are willing to do the work, they should have some say about how the work will be done. Too much lock step runs good volunteers away.

> **"The program asks for my input and then doesn't use it."** Experienced volunteers are generally responsible people and when asked to provide input to the program, they often do. This is particularly true when it comes to scheduling their volunteer time. If you ask the question and the volunteer takes time to answer you, use the information they give you.

### Example
Rex is a retiree and an avid golfer. For the past two years he has volunteered at a number of professional golf matches in his state as a score keeper, a ball marker, and as a marshal for crowd control. He received a letter

inviting him to volunteer at a week long golf tournament. The letter included a form for him to complete and return outlining which days and times were best for him to volunteer. Rex returned the form promptly saying he could work any time Monday through Friday, but he could not work on the weekend. Several weeks later, Rex got a letter from the Volunteer Coordinator telling him he was scheduled to work from 10:00 a.m. to 5:30 p.m. on Saturday and Sunday. Rex said he might have understood it if someone had called him to discuss the schedule. Instead he was just told when to be there, as if they hadn't even read his reply. To himself Rex said, "It would serve them right if I just didn't show up."

➤ **They are bored.** People lose interest when they are no longer being challenged. Volunteers who have been doing the same job month after month get bored and begin looking for more satisfying ways to use their time. Unless the volunteer program recognizes this tendency and gives volunteers an opportunity to grow and to move into other jobs, good volunteers will leave and take their time and talents elsewhere. Just because a person does a job well doesn't mean she wouldn't enjoy a change of pace. Give these good volunteers a chance to move into leadership positions or another aspect of your program. Don't take them for granted. Be particularly cautious with volunteers who are initially satisfied with entry level jobs. Periodically when you thank them for their work, ask if there is another job they would like to learn.

➤ **"No one cares about solving problems in this organization and I'm tired of fighting."** Volunteers who bring problems to the attention of their supervisors expect to have them addressed. To listen to a problem and do nothing about it or to dismiss it as unimportant, discounts the value of the volunteer. If the volunteer is concerned enough about the problem to tell the bosses, there is probably something to it. This is especially true if more than one volunteer has raised the issue. Whether the problem is one of no supplies, equipment not being repaired, poor organization, or policy decisions, the program stands to lose a good volunteer when it ignores the problem. Ignore the problem and the volunteer will go away, often for good.

## Example

Kayla is an energetic and enthusiastic girls' youth group leader. She works hard with the girls in her group to plan activities and encourages them to participate in the larger organization's activities as well. A tri-county mother/daughter weekend camp out had been planned for all the younger groups, including Kayla's group. Kayla's girls were excited. However, as the weekend drew near, there was indecision at the parent organization whether the camp out would begin on Friday night or Saturday morning and whether fathers could attend if mother's were not available. Kayla's group had two girls whose parents were divorced and whose fathers had custody of them.

Kayla attended two meetings scheduled to resolve these issues. Neither meeting resolved them. Finally, the Monday before the camp out the decision was made that the camp out would begin on Friday evening. It was decided that fathers attending would create too much of a problem, especially since the camp had only bathroom facilities for girls. Kayla's girls, whose fathers had custody of them, were disappointed and Kayla herself was frustrated. Had these decisions been made earlier, she and her assistant leader could have presented them in a way that would have allowed the girls to make other plans, such as asking aunts or grandmothers to go with them instead of their dads. After the several incidents of this type, Kayla realized that lack of advance planning and delaying decisions to the last minute were the norm with the parent organization's leadership. Gradually she withdrew from activities, leaving the group in the hands of the assistant leader.

➤ **They're tired of doing the dirty jobs.** Be careful how often you give volunteers dirty jobs to do. No matter how committed the volunteer may be, too many back to back difficult jobs will burn out even the best of volunteers. Be sensitive to the impact of hard jobs on individuals.

### *Example*

Linda had been a volunteer income tax counselor in a community program for several years. Besides helping people prepare their tax returns, she also taught other volunteers how to do the job. Periodically she was asked by the program administrator to correct errors made by other volunteers. She was good at this and also took time to go back and explain the errors to the counselors who had made the mistakes. Gradually, every error was being referred to Linda to handle. She discussed the problem with the program administrator, but there was little change. Finally, she became disgusted and said, "I"m out of here. I just can't do this anymore."

The old saying, "Don't ride your best horse to death," applies in this case. Avoiding the situation, because after all she does the work so well, is difficult. Build on the long range benefits of keeping your best volunteers by not over-loading them.

Although certainly not all inclusive, these are the major reasons good volunteers quit. By getting to know their volunteers as individuals and listening to them, leaders can anticipate volunteers' disenchantment with the program before it occurs. It is far easier to prevent a volunteer's quitting than to change his mind once he has decided to quit. An experienced volunteer who knows you and your program is far more valuable than several new volunteers. And keeping volunteers is easier than recruiting and developing new ones.

# 13

# WHO KEEPS VOLUNTEERING

**In general people who continue to volunteer have four things in common.**

**1)** They care about the cause or the people the program serves.

**2)** They believe what they are doing makes a difference.

**3)** They enjoy what they do.

**4)** And they feel their work is appreciated.

These factors apply regardless of the type of volunteer program: volunteer firefighters, USO volunteers, soup kitchen volunteers, or volunteer tour guides at historic sites. People will not continue to give their time and abilities unless these factors are present.

Although the cause or the people a volunteer program serves may not be the first reason volunteers sign up, ultimately volunteers who stay become committed to the goals of the program. They believe in the value of what the program does and they feel they are a part of the program's overall success in reaching its goals. These volunteers do more than just talk about the program. They put their heart, time and energy where their mouth is.

Volunteers who stay know without question the work they do makes a difference. They see their work as an integral part of a larger whole. In some volunteer programs it is easy for volunteers to see this connection. In most programs, though, the Volunteer Coordinator or volunteer supervisor can enhance this connection by showing and telling volunteers how their work fits into the big picture. Share the successes of your program with all your volunteers. Successful volunteer programs are team efforts.

**People must enjoy what they do as volunteers or they will not continue to do it.** This means matching jobs to volunteers. One size does not fit all and it is essential to find the job that best suits the individual volunteer's skills and interests. The work environment, and particularly the people they work with, can make even difficult jobs enjoyable.

When volunteers know their work is appreciated by the organization, they are not only more committed to the volunteer program, they often volunteer more time. It takes only a few minutes to thank volunteers personally for their good work. Thank volunteers often and be specific about their individual contributions. To the volunteer, this appreciation is priceless and it keeps them coming back to volunteer. Make this thank you personal and sincere.

# 14

# VOLUNTEER COORDINATOR

Every program which uses volunteers needs a Volunteer Coordinator to tailor the volunteer program to the organization and to pull together the resources and the people. This may be a paid position, but more often it, too, is a volunteer job. Although some organizations have several people who are responsible for volunteers, one person should be designated as the primary Volunteer Coordinator or the Volunteer Committee Chairman. As the old adage goes, "When everyone is responsible, no one is responsible." To clarify the role of the Volunteer Coordinator a sample job description is useful.

## Sample job description for a Volunteer Coordinator

The Community Food Bank Volunteer Coordinator is responsible for recruiting, training, and organizing volunteer support for the food bank. Collects input from section managers to determine what work needs to be done when and then assigns volunteers accordingly. Regularly coordinates with section managers to adjust volunteer numbers and schedules, as required, and to resolve problems with volunteers on the job. Reports monthly to the Community Food Bank Chairman the number of volunteers and total hours of volunteer work, as well as any significant changes or upcoming special programs. Collects and provides feedback as necessary to section managers and volunteers on the food bank program as a whole.

Job descriptions will vary depending upon the organization and its relative focus on the use of volunteers. Management and the Volunteer Coordinator must be in agreement on the direction the volunteer program will take. For example, nothing is more frustrating to an energetic Volunteer Coordinator than to launch forth into an enthusiastic program to recruit more volunteers, only to find that management really doesn't want many more volunteers — it only wants the present volunteers to be better trained and more productive.

**Volunteer Coordinator is not a job for the timid or for those most comfortable in orderly administrative settings.** Unfortunately in some organizations, Volunteer Coordinator is an additional duty assigned on a random basis, much like the car pool coordinator or Christmas party organizer. The Volunteer Coordinator establishes the climate for your volunteer program and personality style does make a difference. Extroverts, who are comfortable talking with strangers face to face and on the telephone, are good candidates for Volunteer Coordinator. A high energy level, good organizational skills, and an understanding of the overall goals and policies of the organization are vital. A Volunteer Coordinator who is not fully committed to the organization and the use of volunteers or who is looking for the path of least resistance will produce a mediocre program, at best. Management must understand these points in selecting the Volunteer Coordinator.

### Example

Tinesha was an energetic young college graduate who coordinated the recreation programs for a community youth organization. She supervised the volunteer program, as well as several part time paid staff members. Tinesha had a clear vision of where her program was headed and how it would grow. Her enthusiasm was contagious with the volunteers and the young people her program served. She was often there working side by side with volunteers, especially when they were just starting out. Open to new ideas from volunteers, she often increased program offerings based on their recommendations. She was quick to praise volunteers and patient with those who were struggling. After two years on the job, Tinesha left to become a full time mother.

Tinesha was replaced by Rick, another young college graduate with a similar background. Rick is a hard worker, but he seldom talks to the volunteers. If a volunteer is leading a program, Rick considers it covered and never comes to check. He is reluctant to ask volunteers to do more, accepting instead the status quo. Older volunteers seem to intimidate Rick. Gradually volunteers begin leaving the program. Rick feels overwhelmed, as he and the paid staff members have to cover more and more activities previously led by volunteers. The volunteer base has been seriously eroded before management recognizes their Volunteer Coordinator, Rick, is the problem.

Successful Volunteer Coordinators and management must be attuned to the volunteer climate within their organization. Just because an individual is designated as the Volunteer Coordinator does not automatically mean they can do the job.

**Good Volunteer Coordinators are cheerleaders, minus megaphones and uniforms.** They know how to talk with and listen to people. As a result, they are able to attract and encourage volunteers. While it may not be possible 100% of the time, successful Volunteer Coordinators work hard to be enthusiastic and to maintain a cheerful, optimistic attitude with volunteers. They take time to get to know people, to wish them happy birthday, or to inquire about the health of an elderly parent, for example. As one long time volunteer said about Margaret Brock, a well loved coordinator of volunteers for the Atlanta History Center, "She was always smiling, thanking you, and generally making what you were doing really pleasurable." Volunteer Coordinators set the tone for programs and you can't do this from behind a desk or in an office on the other side of town. You must be visible and involved. Like canoes, volunteer programs are by their very nature somewhat unstable since no volunteer is required to work. Volunteers work because they want to. If they aren't enjoying what they are doing, they don't keep coming. If you aren't regularly checking on how things are going and making adjustments, the canoe will capsize leaving you to wonder what went wrong.

**Successful volunteer programs are not one man shows.** I'll do it myself may be the easy way in the beginning, but it will ultimately stymie the growth of a volunteer program. To capitalize on volunteers you must have teamwork. Volunteer Coordinators, who can divide jobs into smaller tasks and delegate these, find the workload shared and their time freed for other work. Putting together teams is a skill developed through experience. You have to sort volunteers according to abilities and personalities. Anticipate differences in personality styles. Assign people to different teams if a personality clash appears evident. Be flexible enough to fine tune team composition as people get to know one another and become more proficient at their skills. No team should be permanent.

Even though the Volunteer Coordinator may have more in common with some volunteers than with others, it is imperative that all volunteers feel they are important to the program. A perception that some volunteers are being treated preferentially will not only cause grumbling and dissension, it will lose volunteers. Particularly in volunteer programs which have been in existence for a number of years, there is a tendency to have the A team and the B team. The A team is the small group of dedicated volunteers, often including the Volunteer Coordinator, who have been with the program a long time and who generally call the shots. The B team is everyone else. The fact is the A team cannot survive without the B team. If there is no movement of people in and out of the A team, many members of the B team will become discouraged and leave. By working to include the B team in sharing information, recognition and ideas, the Volunteer Coordinator can defuse this potential bomb before it becomes a problem.

**After enthusiasm, probably the most valuable trait for a Volunteer Coordinator is patience, and on occasion, the ability to instill patience into management.** Usually things do not happen fast in volunteer programs, because it takes time to coordinate the information and the people to get a job done or to change how things are being done. Losing your patience, either with yourself or with volunteers, is counterproductive. Whatever job you need done, the right person will show up although not always exactly when you would like to have them. Similarly if a change needs to be made, give it time to take effect.

Volunteer programs grow and change over time. It is unrealistic, and indeed impossible, to stay the same. Just as Volunteer Coordinators work to develop and expand the capabilities of their volunteers, so they must groom others to be Volunteer Coordinators. Often future Volunteer Coordinators are successful team leaders, provided the team leader is focused on people rather than on the product or the process.

**The Volunteer Coordinator makes or breaks a volunteer program.** Management must understand this when selecting an individual for the job. Management must also give the Volunteer Coordinator support, encouragement, and the necessary resources to capitalize on volunteer talent.

# 15

# IN THE FINAL ANALYSIS...

In the final analysis, volunteer programs are what you make them. There are great people out there with exceptional talents who are willing to give their time as volunteers. They are looking for programs that make a difference, are well organized, and will value their contributions. These people thrive on the energy generated by volunteering. Volunteering is a way for individuals to be part of something doing good work that is much larger than themselves.

*Together we can do far more for others than we can alone — and we can have a good time doing it.*

# Notes

# APPENDIX A:

## BUSINESS SUPPORTED VOLUNTEER PROGRAMS

As businesses increasingly recognize their role in the community, more and more are becoming involved in volunteer programs. These partnerships can be beneficial not only to the community program supported, but to the business as well. Benefit to the community is obvious. More subtle is the pay off to the business. Employees get a change of pace from their regular job, a chance to feel they are making a difference, and the added bonus of what one volunteer calls, psychic energy, which can then be brought back to the workplace. Successful business supported volunteer programs have several things in common.

**Management, from the top level down to the first line supervisor, is fully committed to the volunteer program.** Generally if the big boss supports it and periodically asks questions about it, the rest of management will fall in line. The best way to demonstrate this is for the boss to participate occasionally as a volunteer. Smart managers and supervisors will join the boss and participate themselves. This is the classic case of do as I do being more effective than do as I say. In addition, asking for periodic reports from supervisors on how many employees in their section are volunteering makes the volunteer program part of the business plan rather than a nice to have, but expendable adjunct.

**To be effective, businesses must give their employees work time to volunteer.** That is, volunteers must be paid for the time they volunteer. While this may sound contradictory, if the business is volunteering, then the business should give its time to the program. This is not the same as an individual volunteering his own time. Some businesses actually believe they are supporting volunteer programs when they simply encourage their employees to volunteer. Employees who volunteer during their free time are often a credit to the business they work for, but this is not the same as a business supported volunteer program.

**In selecting a volunteer program to support, businesses would be wise to consult their employees about what the employees might like to do.** After all, if people enjoy what they are doing, they are more likely to do a good job and to continue participating. Just because the boss thinks volunteering at the reptile house at the zoo is a great idea, doesn't mean his employees will share his enthusiasm. Although consensus is not essential, some employee input is useful before deciding which program your company will support.

**In addition to encouraging employees to volunteer while they are being paid for working, employers need to make it easy to get to and from the volunteer program site.** One way to do this is to develop a volunteer partnership with a program close to your plant, for example, a near by public school. It can also be done by providing transportation to and from the volunteer program. In some situations, providing transportation may give businesses better control of their volunteers to ensure that they do in fact work at the volunteer program and then return to work after their volunteer time is completed. The specifics depend on the business and the volunteer program. In nearly every case, though, it is incumbent on the volunteer program to let the business know how many volunteers worked and, sometimes, who worked by name. This feedback is essential whether the volunteers work individually once every week or in a large group only on a specified day.

**Businesses which give their employees bonuses can reinforce their volunteer programs** by increasing bonuses to employees who volunteer over those whose work is equal except they do not volunteer. Although it is not the same as a business supported volunteer program, businesses that wish to encourage their employees to volunteer in the community as individuals on their own time, can also use bonuses to reward employees who volunteer. To avoid contention, though, it is important to have an independent way of checking whether an employee really volunteers or has merely signed up and never done any work.

**While not a new idea, people do best those things the boss checks.** Business supported volunteer programs are no exception. Supervisors, who know which of their employees volunteer, are in an excellent position to reinforce and encourage participation.

### Example

"Don, how's the book sorting at Goodwill going? Are there enough volunteers showing up to get the job done?. . . I sure appreciate your good work with this program. It really makes Associated Industries a part of our community."

**Business supported volunteer programs can have tremendous impact provided management remains committed.** Too often businesses enter agreements to provide volunteers for organizations, start out with great enthusiasm and involvement, and then fail to sustain the commitment. Over time the volunteer program goes from being a priority to routine to a commitment in name only. Finally the business is no longer providing people as volunteers, it is only donating outdated equipment or possibly money. Money is important, but it is not the same as volunteers. Money cannot buy volunteers. This not only fails the organization to which the volunteer commitment was made, it gives the business a poor reputation. An individual, who makes a commitment to volunteer and then fails to follow through, can usually survive the negative reputation. A business, on the other hand, has a lot more to lose.

The potential of business supported volunteer programs to make our communities better for everyone is unlimited provided the business, not just individual employees, is committed to making the partnership a success.

# APPENDIX B:
## LIABILITY AND INSURANCE CONSIDERATIONS

In today's lawsuit prone society, many organizations are reluctant to become involved with volunteers because they are afraid something might happen and they could be sued. Organizations paralyzed by fear cannot hope to excel. While nothing in life is totally risk free, free floating anxiety about what might happen with volunteers is largely unnecessary. Risks can be controlled by controlling the kind of work you ask volunteers to do and by providing adequate supervision for volunteers. Not many volunteer programs are going to make volunteers heavy equipment operators or surgical assistants. Look at what your volunteers will actually be doing.

Potential liability is another reason to start new volunteers in low risk entry level jobs, advancing them to more responsible and more complicated tasks only after you get to know them and their style. For example, you probably wouldn't ask a person you had just met to run an errand in you personal car. For the same reason, it's not a good idea to put a new volunteer behind the wheel of your organization's van transporting people. In some cases training will be necessary for individuals to move beyond entry level jobs, but be certain the training is actually needed as opposed to being an overzealous cover your rear requirement. Volunteers are quick to recognize the difference between necessary training and an implication that they are not trusted.

If your organization already has liability insurance, it is probably a good idea to discuss the addition of volunteers to your workforce with your insurance carrier. Be sure to tell them up front, though, exactly what your volunteers will be doing, how many hours they will be working, and the limits and supervision you will use with them. Otherwise insurance carriers can jump to conclusions about the something that might happen. Similarly, you may also want to talk about the use of volunteers with your legal advisor, if you have one.

Insurance is available to cover volunteers injured on the job and to protect your organization from lawsuits resulting from injuries caused by volunteers. An excellent resource on this subject is Am I Covered For . . .? A Guide to Insurance for Non-Profit Organizations, by Mary L. Lai, Terry S. Chapman, and Elmer L. Steinbock, (Consortium for Human Services, 1992).

Make an honest assessment of your current or proposed volunteer program and the risk to which it exposes your organization. Just because someone heard about a similar program in Timbuktu that was sued for $100,000 because of a volunteer, doesn't mean your organization will have the same problem. It also doesn't mean the courts actually found the program in question liable or awarded a $100,000 settlement.

*If you are unwilling to take any risk at all, you cannot expect to reap the benefits of the wide ranging talents of volunteers.*

## ABOUT THE AUTHOR

With over 30 years of experience in volunteer programs, Jo Rusin understands volunteering from both worker and management perspectives. She began as a youth program leader with the YWCA in 1965 and has since volunteered with public schools, a hospital, the American Red Cross, the YMCA, Girl Scouts, and Boy Scouts of America. While serving in the U.S. Army, Jo worked on the Army's transition from the draft to the current all volunteer force. She is currently a volunteer swimming and first aid instructor with the American Red Cross, Volunteer Coordinator for Golden Retriever Rescue of Atlanta, and a volunteer tutor and mentor with the Atlanta Public Schools. Jo is a 1996 recipient of the Golden Apple Award which recognizes the Atlanta Public Schools' most outstanding volunteers.